TALK OF THE TOWN

TALK OF THE TOWN

The Place Names in our Language

By

CECIL HUNT

LONDON : HERBERT JENKINS

First published by
Herbert Jenkins Ltd.
3 Duke of York Street,
London, S.W.1.
1951

Printed in Great Britain by Butler & Tanner Ltd., Frome and London

FOREWORD

MANY readers of my *Dictionary of Word Makers* have been so kind as to suggest a companion volume of literary and book lovers' reference on the place names in our language.

Such a book was in fact visualized and started as a companion and complementary work before the publication of *Word Makers*. For I had found myself and my friends making frequent use of place names and products without sensing their often fascinating association, or even being sure of their location.

When I placed upon the tiny counter of a village post-office letters addressed to Camembert and Gorgonzola, the post-mistress said: "But they're cheeses!" They were no more to her; and, I suspect, to most of us.

Other writers and book-lovers will, I hope, share my pleasure and increase the richness of their writing and reading, and the pleasure of their conversation, by this dictionary of the place names that have brought tradition, life and colour to our vivid, everyday language.

It would be simple to extend this book indefinitely, but I have tried in the entries to keep the accent upon frequently used allusions and to elucidate references that are continually met in ordinary, catholic reading and conversation.

I have not attempted to include the numerous misnomers, the Jerusalem artichoke, Guernsey lily, Turkey rhubarb and the like. Those who wish can pursue them in many existing reference books. I have ignored the many food and dish names which, while they carry a location, are no longer specifically associated therewith, or even especially procurable in the district of their alleged origin.

I gladly record my thanks to the following for their kind assistance in supplying and correcting information embodied in this book: Henry Poole & Co., Savile Row; Commune di Gorgonzola; the Town Clerks of Caerphilly (and Councillor H. P. Richards), Llanelly and Helston; The Bell, Stilton; Instituto Nazionale per il Commercio Estero, Rome; Alex. Ferguson, Ltd., Edinburgh; John Harvey & Sons, Ltd., Bristol; Hugh M. Stephens, Editor, *Ridley's Wine and Spirit Trade Circular*; the Italian Chamber of Commerce; Arthur Wiggins.

At least I can claim with Boswell: "I have sometimes been obliged to run half over London in order to fix a date correctly; which, when I had accomplished, I well knew would obtain me no praise, though a failure would have been to my discredit."

Fortunately, a writer's life is enlivened and restored by the kind letters of readers.

The pursuit has been fascinating and I hope that readers will find equal pleasure in these rewarding and informing excursions into geography and history.

CECIL HUNT

GREAT DUNMOW,
ESSEX.

TALK OF THE TOWN

Aberdeen of Aberdeen Terrier. Aberdeen, the granite city and port in the east of Scotland, at the mouth of the River Dee, is a great commercial centre and fishing port. It is a university and cathedral city. The name Aberdeen terrier was applied to what is more strictly the Scottish terrier because the strain was once raised extensively in the city.

Abruzzi of the Abruzzi Sheepdog. Abruzzi and Molise is an Eastern province of Italy with an Adriatic seaboard. The fertile and well-watered valleys of the Appennines support a large agricultural trade, together with vineyards and extensive sheep farms.

The Abruzzi sheepdog, used extensively for centuries in central Italy, is known also as the Maremma sheepdog, from the marshy Maremma region in southern Tuscany. The breed has only recently been introduced into Britain.

The dogs are white—with a few exceptions which show biscuit or light fawn on the head—are substantial and appear to the layman reminiscent of the golden retriever and Labrador in form.

Academy of Academy, academic, etc. The original Academy was the garden near Athens, where Plato taught. It was reputed to have been founded by the hero Academus, or Akademos. The Academy was noted for its olive groves and included a gymnasium. Plato divided his academy into three schools—the Old, the Middle and the New. He was buried near the olive grove, which afterwards became noted for the teachings there of other philosophers.

Accad of Accadian. Accad is one of the four cities mentioned in *Gen. x. 10* as having been founded by Nimrod in the land of Shinar. The others were Babel (*q.v.*), Erech and Calneh. The sacred texts of Assyria and Babylonia were written in Accadian, a language preserved in cuneiform inscriptions. Accad, or Akkad, which means mountain land, was near the Euphrates.

Aceldama of Aceldama. The Aramaic word aceldama, meaning the field of blood, has become a synonym thereof, and of a place of slaughter. It is mentioned by this name in *Acts i. 19* for what is called in *Matt. xxvii. 7–8* "the potter's field, to bury strangers in." It was renamed after Judas had bought it with the money received for the betrayal of Christ. "Now this man purchased a field with the reward of iniquity; and falling headlong, he burst asunder in the midst, and all his bowels gushed out. And it was known unto all the dwellers at Jerusalem; insomuch as that field is called in their proper tongue, Aceldama, that is to say, The field of blood" (*Acts i. 18–19*).

Tradition claims that the field was situated near the vale of Hinnom, a deep ravine between Mount Zion and the Hill of Evil Council, so called because there, in the house of Caiaphas, the rulers decided to put Christ to death.

Adullam of Adullamite. Adullam, the ancient royal city of the Canaanites, was in the valley of Elah and was the scene of David's victory over Goliath (*1 Sam. xvii. 4*). The cave of Adullam, some two miles south of the city, was the refuge of David and his followers.

9

The term Adullamite, strictly denoting a dweller in the city, is often applied to seceders from prominent parties and beliefs, who gather about them discontents. John Bright, in 1866, named as Adullamites the adherents to Lowe and Horsman, who seceded from the Liberal party. The Biblical passage (*1 Sam. xxii. 1–2*) refers to the gathering under the captaincy of David of those in distress and discontent.

Afghanistan of the Afghan Hound.

Afghanistan, the country to the northwest of India, between Persia and the U.S.S.R., has been the home of the Afghan Hound for centuries. There this speedy and hardy dog is much used in hunting, even for big game. Though common to the whole country the breed was particularly found in Balkh, the capital, hence its alternative name, the Balkh Hound.

It is similar in outline to the Saluki (pron. *Saloogi*), but its long, silky coat gives the Afghan hound a pantalooned appearance. It has been known in Britain for nearly half a century.

Airedale of Airedale Terrier. York-

shire, the north-eastern maritime county, is the largest in England and is divided into the North, East and West Ridings, or thirdings.

Among its famous dales is Airedale, which area was the breeding place of the Airedale terrier, a cross between the Otterhound and a black and tan. The breed, which is popular as a companion and as a guard dog, has been in existence about a century. It was first called a Broken-haired Terrier.

The Yorkshire terrier, one of the smallest toy breeds, was common to the whole county, and particularly the West Riding, where it was bred by miners for ratting and other pursuits in which its gameness and pocket size were an advantage.

Alabastron of Alabaster. Pliny

(24–79), in his *Natural History*, a work

of thirty-seven books, mostly published posthumously, says that the ancient alabaster was named from the Egyptian town Alabastron, near where it was found. It was a hard, marble-like lime carbonate obtained from stalagmites and stalactites and used for ornamental purposes and luxury goods. Reference is made in the Gospels to "a woman having an alabaster box of ointment of spikenard very precious" (*Mark xiv. 3*).

The alabaster of to-day is a hydrated sulphate of lime, appreciably softer than the ancient form.

Albi of Albigenses. The Albi-

genses, or Catharists, were a substantial heretical sect in France during the 12th to 14th centuries. They objected to all Catholic doctrines and organization and were of sufficient strength to require condemnation at various great Councils of the Church and to have a crusade preached against them and an inquisition set up when Papal attempts at extirpation and conciliation failed.

The heretics derived their name from Albi, the French town in the department of Tarn, which is near the Spanish frontier. Here their persecutions began.

Albi, which is the seat of an archbishop and has a substantial trade in linen, wine, etc., is north of Toulouse, which is in the same department.

Alhambra of Alhambra. Many

millions of people have visited, and many still visit, a theatre, music-hall or cinema called The Alhambra, without knowing the derivation of its name. It originated in the palace and citadel of the Moorish monarchs in Granada in the 13th century. It was a place of great beauty, luxury and wealth. The name derives from *Kal' at-al-hamra*, the red castle, so called because of the colour of the walls.

There is a town Alhambra in Los Angeles, California.

Alabanda of Almandine. Alabanda, a city in Caria, is, through Alabandine, the origin of Almandine, the red garnet, or Carbuncle. It contains oxides of iron and aluminium and varies in colour from deep crimson to violet red. The word carbuncle is derived from the Latin, *carbunculus*, a small coal. These garnets are now mined in India, and Jaipur, in Rajputana, is a noted cutting and distributing centre.

Caria, with which Alamandines were originally associated, is a maritime province of Asia Minor. The country, which was conquered by Alexander the Great and became part of the Roman Empire, is now embodied in the Turkish Empire. Smyrna (Izmir) and Ephesus are in the Caria province.

Alsace-Lorraine of the Alsatian dog. Alsace-Lorraine was, between 1871 and the First World War, in the possession of Germany. To that fact must be attributed the name of the Alsatian dog which is more correctly called the German Shepherd dog or Deutsch Schaferhund. It is, in fact, called by one of these names in almost every country where it is known, except Britain.

The breed, which has long been popular in Germany, appeared in this country at the beginning of this century, but was prejudiced by the German associations, particularly when, as it became more generally known, the First World War was imminent. After the war it appeared as the Alsatian Wolfhound, a similarly handicapping appellation because the wolf-like appearance, together with some accidents with erratic, unacclimatized specimens, increased public apprehensions and resulted in a "bad press."

The breed has surmounted its unfortunate advent to this country, largely because of its handsome appearance, its proved faithfulness and its magnificent work as trained guides for the blind, as police dogs and in military employment. In obedience and field trials it has reached high levels of intelligence.

It is of literary interest that the name Alsatia was, up to the end of the 17th century, given to the Whitefriars district of London, between Fleet Street and the Thames. It was a sanctuary for debtors and other lawbreakers, taking its name, in this association, from Alsace which had long been a disputed territory similarly exploited by those seeking to elude the law.

Amboyna of Amboyna wood. The finely marked wood of the Asiatic Amboyna tree is named from Amboyna island. The name is sometimes spelt Amboina. It is Dutch territory in the Moluccas, between New Guinea on the east and Celebes on the west. There is a Government Residency and the island has an area of 266 square miles. It was a centre of the spice trade.

There is a British island of Amboina in the South China Sea, north-west of British North Borneo.

Andalusia of Andalusite. The anhydrous silicate of alumina which gives the brilliant gem, andalusite, is named from the former province of Spain, Andalusia, divided in 1833 into the eight provinces of Cadiz, Cordova, Granada, Jaen, Huelva, Malaga, Almena and Seville. It was the southern province, with Mediterranean seaboard.

The gem is now more frequently mined in Ceylon and Brazil. There is an opaque variety, alternatively known as the chiastrolite, which reveals intricate patterns when cut and polished.

Angora of Angora goat, rabbit and cat (also **Angola**). Angora (Ankara) was an ancient town of Asia Minor, scene of a great battle between the Turks and the Tartars in the 15th century.

Under the new Turkish regime it

has superseded Constantinople (Istanbul) which is 200 miles to the west-north-west. For centuries Angora was noted for its goats, which had unusually long and valuable silky hair. When manufactured this product is known as mohair. Long, silky hair is the characteristic of the Angora rabbit and cat, though these animals have not the same intimate association with the city.

The name Angora, now renamed Ankara, is frequently corrupted to Angola.

Angostura of Angostura Bitters. Renamed Cuidad Bolivar, the city formerly and still better known as Angostura, is capital of Bolivar, in the republic of Venezuela, South America. It is on the south bank of the Orinoco. It is an episcopal see and trades in cattle and live stock, sugar, tobacco, etc.

Angostura bitters are derived from the bark of an indigenous tree, *Cusparia febrifuga*, of the order of *Rutaceæ*. The product is used extensively in drugs, particularly for its tonic effect. Its value as a febrifuge, or fever reducer, is said to be slight.

Apollinaris of Apollinaris Water. The source and the name-giver of this alkaline mineral water was the Apollinaris spring in the Ahr Valley, in the Rhine Province of Germany. It flanks the Belgian frontier.

Arabia of The Arabian Nights, Bird, Arabesque, etc. The connection of Arabia with one of the classic collections of short stories is that most of the stories in *The Arabian Nights' Entertainments*, or *The Thousand and One Nights*, are Arabian in character and possibly in origin.

Arabia is the vast, most westerly peninsula in Asia.

The device of tale-telling, the king who killed his wives on the morning after their marriage until one, Scheherazade, saved her life by the stories she told him, is Persian in origin.

The collection of stories was made known in Europe by the 18th-century translation of Antoine Galland. The famous English translations are by Sir Richard Burton, dated 1840 and 1885–8.

Scheherazade is the subject of a symphonic suite by Rimsky-Korsakov (1844–1908).

The Arabian Bird was the phœnix, possessing fabulous qualities, including an ability to immolate itself upon its self-ignited nest and to rise from the ashes. It is mentioned in *Cymbeline*, i. 6.

Arabesque is an architectural term applied to Arabian and Moorish architecture, and its characteristic decoration. In music an Arabesque is an ornamental melodic figure.

The term "Arab" for a street urchin in earlier times, and still less widely surviving, is a reference to the nomadic, restless characteristics of the Arabs.

An Arab stallion is regarded as the prototype of equine virility and spirit.

Arauco of Araucaria. Arauco, the city and maritime province of Chile, is concerned with agriculture and forestry and has given its name to the genus of trees, *Araucaria*. The most widely known is the Chilean Pine, or Monkey Puzzle, which flourishes in southern Britain and Europe. It is the *araucaria imbricata*. It is usually raised in this country from imported seed and seldom flowers. It is an important timber tree in Chile, yielding soft, yellow, resinous wood.

Other araucarias flourish in the southern hemisphere, but are seldom seen north of the equator.

Arcadia of Arcadian. Arcadia was a mountain district of the central Peloponnese. It has many associations with Greek mythology and in certain accounts was named as the birthplace of Zeus. Hermes and Pan were originally Arcadian deities.

According to Virgil, its people, who had resisted Dorian and Spartan aggression, inhabited a land of idyllic rustic peace and simplicity.

Sir Philip Sidney (1554–86) used the name in this connection in his *Arcadia*, which appeared posthumously, as did all his works, in 1590.

The expression passed into general usage and Lionel Monckton utilized the same theme of rustic simplicity in his popular and frequently revived musical play *The Arcadians*, first produced in 1909.

Armageddon of Armageddon. The use of the word Armageddon as a synonym of supreme disaster or vast conflict between nations, derives from the reference in *Rev. xvi. 16*. At the climax of the conflict between the powers of good and evil the foul spirits are gathered "into a place called in the Hebrew tongue Armageddon" (*xvi. 16*). The name derives from the mount of Megiddo, the place of troops, a Canaanite royal city conquered by Joshua (*xii. 21*).

Arras of Arras. The ancient cathedral city of Arras is the capital of the French department of Pas de Calais. It is 120 miles north of Paris, on the river Scarpe. It has an important textile industry, together with agricultural produce and implements, etc. A decisive battle was fought at Arras in the First World War.

For many centuries it was famous for its tapestry, which took the name of the city. The tapestry was frequently hung round the walls of a house, sufficiently far from them to give hiding-place to an intruder or eavesdropper.

In this connection the arras is frequently mentioned in history and in literature. It was the natural hiding-place of spies, plotters and murderers.

Prince, to Falstaff: "Go, hide thee behind the arras . . ." *1 Henry IV, ii. 4*.

Ascot of Ascot. The famous circular racecourse at Ascot is 6 miles south-west of Windsor, in Berkshire.

The Ascot meetings are important social events, frequently enjoying Royal patronage. King Edward VII took an active interest in the development of the Ascot course in 1902. The Ascot Gold Cup, 2½ miles, was instituted in 1807. Between the years 1845–53 it was known as "The Emperor's Plate."

Asti of Asti Spumante. The ancient cathedral city of Asti, in the north-west Italian province of Piedmont, was famous for its pottery as long ago as 400 B.C. The name is incorporated in that of the sparkling Italian wine, Asti Spumante, which has international reputation.

Piedmont produces the grapes used for the famous Vermouth di Torina and other wines of the district include Barolo, Freisa, Nebiolo and Cortese, the latter a straw-coloured wine with greenish shades.

Astrakan of Astrakan. The Astrakan province in the south-east of the U.S.S.R. flanks the Volga and the capital is on its delta at the Caspian Sea. It is an ancient city whose commerce has been largely extended by the increased use of petroleum.

It has given its name to the tight, curled fur, formerly much used, and still used to some extent, for the facings of heavy overcoats, etc. It is obtained from the skin of very young Persian lambs.

Astrakan claims a large export of the delicacy caviare—the roe of sturgeons and other fish—caught in the Caspian and Black Seas.

Athenæum of Athenæum. The famous school or academy founded by Hadrian in the 1st century B.C. was called the Athenæum, after Athene, the Greek goddess of wisdom, identified with the Roman Minerva.

The Athenæum stood upon the Capitoline Hill in Rome.

The Athenæum, one of London's most distinguished and learned clubs, was established in 1824.

Athens of Attic. Athens, the capital of Attica, gives its name to many illusions still current. The Attic dialect was the Greek spoken by the Athenians and Attic wit or Attic salt was the elegant, refined wit for which the city was famous. The style and idiom of Athens was known as atticism.

The Attic Order is an architectural term applying to a small square column or pillar of any of the five classic Orders: Tuscan, Doric, Ionic, Corinthian and Composite.

The *Attic Nights* of Aulus Gellius (2nd century A.D.) are essays and diaries concerned with Athens, whither the author went from Rome to study philosophy. There were originally twenty books, of which nineteen survive.

Sophocles (496–406 B.C.), one of the three great Attic tragedians, was called the Attic Bee, from the mellifluence of his writings.

The nightingale was known as the Attic bird because of the abundance of nightingales in Attica. Other accounts derive the title from the fact that Philomel, or Philomela, and Procne were daughters of Pandion, a legendary king of Athens. According to Greek accounts Philomel was changed into a swallow and her sister into a nightingale. Latin authors reverse the translation and make Philomel assume the form of the nightingale, by which personal name the bird is frequently referred to in poetry. Ralegh (1552?–1618) says in *The Nymph's Reply to the Passionate Shepherd*, "And Philomel becometh dumb." Samuel Coleridge (1772–1834), in *The Nightingale*, writes of "Philomela's pity-pleading strains."

The attic storey of a house or building was so named because in early times this low storey was raised on small pilasters instead of columns, hence the association with the Attic Order of architecture.

Mount Atlas of Atlantic. The word Atlantic is thought to derive from Mount Atlas, but by some the name is attributed to the mythical Atlantis, an island engulfed by the sea and supposed to lie in the Atlantic, west of the straits of Gibraltar. Other sites have been named for it and it has been the subject of search since classical times.

Mount Atlas was in Libya and the great chain of peaks and plateau lands stretches from Morocco to Tunis.

In Greek mythology Atlas was one of the Titans who, because of his attempts to overthrow Zeus, was compelled by him to support the pillars of the heavens upon his broad shoulders.

Other accounts give Atlas as a King of Mauretania, who, for his lack of hospitality to Perseus, was changed into a mountain.

Mercator, the great cartographer, used the figure of Atlas, with the globe upon his back, on the title page of his 16th-century collection of maps.

Avon of "The Swan of Avon." The title was bestowed upon Shakespeare by Ben Jonson (1572–1637), referring to the Avon of Stratford, Warwicks, Shakespeare's birthplace in 1564.

Axminster of Axminster carpets. The Devon town, on the river Axe, east of Exeter, is of ancient history and stands on the junction of Ikneild Street and the Fosse Way. The carpet industry, for which it was famous, was established in 1755. The carpets were woven by hand, like tapestry.

A characteristic of the early Axminsters was that they were made to order, in one piece, to fit the dimensions of each room. They are tufted and resemble Turkey carpets (*q.v.*).

Chenille Axminsters, patented in Glasgow in 1839, are still largely manufactured there. The chenille (velvety cord) is bound into tufts and is used as the weft in the carpet.

Chenille carpets are also manufactured extensively in Philadelphia (since 1791) and in France.

In the middle of the 19th century

the local Axminster carpet industry was moved to Wilton (*q.v.*), near Salisbury, but just before the Second World War carpet manufacture was restarted in Axminster.

Aylesbury of Aylesbury Ducks. The Buckinghamshire borough of Aylesbury is mentioned in the Domesday Book and is the site of an annual fair recognized by royalty as early as the 13th century. It is a market town and the name a national synonym of quality. Duck breeding is still noted but is less extensive nowadays. Printing is a prominent Aylesbury industry.

B

Babel of Babel. The Tower of Babel, which gives its name to a confusion of sound, an uproar, is recorded in *Gen. xi. 1–9*. After the Deluge the people under Nimrod built a tower in Shinar. It was a tower "whose top may reach unto heaven," and it was to be a rallying point in the vast plain. Then the people all had one language, but at Babel the Lord "did there confound the language of all the earth: and from thence did the Lord scatter them abroad upon the face of all the earth."

Shinar is Babylonia, mentioned also by Isaiah, Daniel, etc.

Babel is mentioned in Milton's *Paradise Lost, xii.*

Babylon of the Whore of Babylon. Babylon, the great capital of the Chaldean empire, is also the mystical city of the Apocalypse (*Rev. xvii. 5*): "Mystery, Babylon the great, the Mother of the harlots and abominations of the earth."

"The Whore of Babylon" was a term applied to the Roman Catholic Church by the early Puritans.

London has been called "The Modern Babylon"—but not lately.

The Hanging Gardens of Babylon, said to have been built by Nebuchadnezzar, were one of the Seven Wonders of the World.

Badminton of Badminton. The seat of the Duke of Beaufort, Badminton Hall, Gloucestershire, gave its name to the familiar game played with rackets and shuttlecocks. It had previously been known in India, but its support as a private game, contrived and developed at Badminton Hall, led to its popularity as a national pastime.

The Badminton Association in England was formed in 1895.

The name Badminton, for a type of claret cup, doubtless originated from the accompaniments of the game in its original British setting.

Balaclava of the Balaclava helmet. The woollen helmet covering the head, neck and shoulders and known as the Balaclava, is named from the site of the Crimean battlefield. The port is on the Black Sea in the south of the Crimea, a few miles from Sebastopol. On the heights between Balaclava and Tchernaya an engagement between the English and the Russians included the famous Charge of the Light Brigade (see Tennyson's *Charge of the Light Brigade*, published December 9, 1854). The helmets were worn on field service.

Balbriggan of Balbriggan. The knitted cotton fabric used in underwear and hosiery, etc., and known as Balbriggan, takes its name from the seaport of its manufacture in Ireland. Balbriggan is 22 miles north-east of Dublin and is noted for its hosiery, linen and woollen manufacturing.

Bagdad of Baldachin or Baldacchino. Bagdad, or Baghdad, the ancient Mohammedan city of Iraq, now a modern university city on the air routes to the East, was known in Italian as Baldacco.

Originally baldachin, or baldaquin, which names derive therefrom, was a rich, ornate brocade associated with the city. It is now, in the word *baldachin* or *baldacchino*, applied to a rich canopy projecting over or suspended above an altar, throne or dais. It is not now necessarily made of tapestry. The term is used frequently in connection with church furnishings. Altars, particularly in churches of the Byzantine style, are adorned with baldacchinos.

The *c* or *cc* in each formation of the word is sounded as *k*.

Balmoral of Balmoral. A type of Scottish cap is particularly known as a Balmoral, but the adjective was also formerly applied to a type of petticoat and to a laced boot.

The name was taken from Balmoral Castle, in Aberdeenshire, Scotland, where the fashions originated or were popularized. It is a residence of the British sovereign and is built in the local granite, commanding a magnificent view of the Dee. The castle was given to Queen Victoria by the Prince Consort.

Banbury of "Ride-a-cock horse to Banbury cross," etc. Banbury, the north Oxfordshire town, is one of the main stock-distributing centres of Britain. It no longer possesses the cross of the nursery rhyme. It was pulled down in Elizabethan times.

A cross still dominates the main street, but it is comparatively modern. It was built in the style of the Eleanor Crosses, though Banbury was not one of the Queen's last resting places. The cross has statues of King Edward VII and King George V.

Banbury cakes are still famous and Tudor ovens can be seen at one of the historic tea shops.

Banbury cheeses, which are mentioned in Shakespeare (*Merry Wives of Windsor, i. 1*), are characterized by their thinness in comparison with most English cheeses. They are about an inch in thickness.

The town was originally associated with a conspicuous cheese-paring, bigoted attitude, so that a Puritan or a bigot was called a "Banbury man." There are several such references in literature. The town was a Puritan stronghold and produced many zealous upholders of the cause, including

a vicar of Banbury who was suspended in 1590 for his views.

Bantam of Bantam, bantam-weight, etc. Bantam, the former seaport of Java, in the Dutch East Indies, 40 miles west of Batavia, was once the seat of the government of Bantam. It is generally assumed to be the place of origin of the Bantam fowl, *Gallus Bankiva*, though some authorities claim that the strain was Japanese in origin.

It is a very small variety, with a silky appearance, and the cock is noted for its spirit and pugnaciousness. This association accounts for the term bantam-weight in boxing (8 st. 6 lb.). The one smaller category is the fly-weight (8 st.).

The name Bantams was given admiringly to battalions raised during the First World War of men below normal physique and size who showed admirable spirit.

Bath of Bath Olivers, Chaps, Chairs, etc. Bath, the chief city of Somerset, is a place of great antiquity. It has magnificently preserved Roman Baths, is noted as a spa and possesses much architectural beauty. The city's crescents particularly are enhanced by its setting in a natural amphitheatre.

Beau Nash, to whom was given the title "The King of Bath," presided, as Master of Ceremonies, over the activities of the famous Assembly Rooms and Pump Room during the first half of the 18th century. Bath, together with Wells, is the seat of an Anglican diocese. It possesses a noble abbey of the perpendicular Gothic period, and a Roman Catholic Priory church.

The city has for centuries been an historic and fashionable centre and is frequently mentioned in literature. It was severely damaged by bombing in the Second World War.

Bath Olivers owe their name to Dr. William Oliver, F.R.S. (1695–

1764), who had a fashionable clientèle in the city, and did much to improve its medical facilities. Dr. Oliver invented the biscuit that bears his name for the benefit of his patients. It still enjoys world popularity.

Bath chaps, or cheeks, are the lower part of pig jaws, associated in a particular curing with the Somerset city. The word chop, used colloquially for cheek, has the same derivation.

The sugared Bath buns are associated with the city, as are the famous Sally Lunns, made by and named after the 18th-century pastry cook of Bath.

Bath chairs, the chairs mounted on wheels and used for invalids, first appeared at this spa.

Bath Post was once the name of a high quality writing paper used by the most fashionable visitors and subsequently copied elsewhere.

Bath shillings were silver tokens issued by Bath tradesmen at the beginning of the 19th century.

An alloy of copper and zinc was once called Bath metal and was probably used by local tradesmen for cheap jewellery, much in the same way as pinchbeck was employed.

Bath Stone is a type of oolitic limestone which quarries easily but hardens on exposure. It is found near Bath and has been used extensively and effectively in the city's architecture.

Bath Brick is not correctly associated specifically with the city. It is alluvial matter pressed into the form of a brick and used for cleaning and polishing metal. It is the product of the Somerset town of Bridgwater and the material is dredged from the river Parret.

The Most Honourable Order of the Bath (1399) is not named from the city but derives its title from the ancient ceremony of bathing, to symbolize purity, at the inauguration of a knight. The rite persisted in this Order up to the time of the Coronation of Charles II in 1661. The Bath King of Arms, who is not a member of the Heralds' College, is occupied only with the Order of the Bath.

Les Baux of Bauxite. Bauxite, the earth compound which is the chief source of aluminium and its salts, takes its name from the district of Les Baux, near Arles, in the south of France, north-west of Marseilles. It is found also in Ireland and the United States.

Bauxite is heat-resisting and is employed in the manufacture of crucibles, ovens, fire-bricks, etc.

Bayeux of the Bayeux Tapestry. Bayeux is a small cathedral city in the Calvados Department of Normandy, almost due south of Bosham, Sussex, which is depicted in the Tapestry. Bayeux is 17 miles north-west of Caen, made memorable in the Second World War, and from which town stone was brought for the building of our cathedrals of Winchester and Canterbury.

The Tapestry, strictly speaking an embroidery as the design is not woven, is 231 ft. long and 20 in. wide. It is primarily a panorama of the invasion and conquest of England. Its exact age and origin are disputed, but it was mentioned in the Bayeux Cathedral Inventory of 1476. It is thought to be more than eight hundred years old, but the colours still retain their freshness and the Tapestry is an incomparable historical record. It is divided into seventy-two sections, with descriptions in Latin. It remained for centuries in the side chapel of Bayeux Cathedral and was hung in the nave once a year on the Feast of Relics, July 1. Napoleon had it brought to Paris in 1803, when invasion of England was imminent.

The first part of the embroidery, which is on coarse linen, depicts the journeyings of Harold, Earl of Wessex, and of his part in the campaign against Brittany. It shows signs of having been joined and suggests the work of various hands. The details of dress, armour, etc., are astonishingly accurate and informative and the scenes remarkably vivid and artistically composed.

Bayonne of Bayonet. The French fortified, cathedral city of Bayonne, in the lower Pyrenees, Gascony, is credited with being the place of invention of the bayonet, in the 17th century. The original form was triangular, with a tapering point. The term bayonet catch, or fitting, still frequently used in connection with mechanical fastenings, derives from its similarity to the original method of fitting the bayonet to the rifle muzzle.

A species of Yucca, with spear or needle-like leaves, is known as the Spanish bayonet.

Beaune of Beaune. The city that gives its name to the famous Burgundian wine, is situated in the east of France, in the Côte d'Or. Its Hospice, which is still the centre of the annual auction of the vintage, dates from 1443.

It was founded by Nicolas Rolin, Chancellor and Minister of Justice. He, wishing "by an auspicious trade to exchange for the heavenly treasures the temporal wealth I owe to God's bounty and from perishable possessions obtain eternal ones; with the consent of the Holy See, thankful of the gifts the Lord has lavished on me, from now and for ever, irrevocably institute and endow a hospital in the city of Beaune for the poor and sick . . ."

The original hospital contained a barn where the crops were gathered and the wine made. Later this part became a ward and other adjoining premises housed the industry. Vineyards which provide some of the choicest wines are among the possessions of the hospice and provide the upkeep of the patients. Many acres have been added by legacy and the most famous vatfuls are called after Nicolas Rolin and other benefactors and bene-

factresses. Until 1851 the Beaune Hospice wines were sold by private contract. This was superseded by annual auction in mid-November, which ceremonial event, with civic patronage, draws thousands of connoisseurs from all over the world. At it the new Chevaliers of the Confrerie du Tastevin are knighted with traditional ritual.

Beaune also manufactures casks, vinegar, white metal, etc.

Bethlem of Bedlam. Bethlem Royal Hospital, now situated at Beckenham, Kent, was originally founded as a priory in 1247. It was known as St. Mary's of Bethlehem and was situated in Bishopsgate, City of London.

It was given to the City Corporation in 1574 and, because of a royal foundation, used as an asylum. In 1676 it moved to Moorfields and in 1815 to Lambeth. At one time in its history it was the scene of much scandalous cruelty and neglect. Inmates were exhibited like animals and allowed abroad when not completely cured. From this period the term bedlam, and the expressions "Bedlam beggars" and "Tom-o-Bedlams," arose.

Hogarth (1697–1764) depicted the horrors and terrors of those times and conditions which brought the corruption of the name into common usage.

John Evelyn (1620–1706) says in his *Diary*: "I stept into Bedlame, where I saw several poore miserable creatures in chaines; one of them was mad with making verses."

Bedlington of Bedlington Terrier. The Northumberland town of Bedlington, on the river Blyth, about 2 miles from its mouth, supports collieries and glass works. The speedy, courageous Bedlington terrier, recognized by the layman by its lamb-like coat, top-knot and flat head, was bred by Bedlington miners for ratting, rabbit coursing and for drawing foxes, otters and badgers. It was given its present name when it achieved wider prominence, just over a century ago. It had previously been called the Rothbury Terrier, after the gypsies of the Rothbury Forest, which lies north-north-west of Bedlington. It was also called the Northern Counties Fox Terrier.

San Benito of Benitoite. At the opening of this century the discovery of a new gem mineral in San Benito County, California, promised the recognition of another semi-precious, if not precious, stone. It was named Benitoite, and the gem varies from white to deep blue in colour. It is a barium titano-silicate. It has not been mined elsewhere and its limitations at the place of its source have prevented its becoming as widely known as its qualities merit.

Bergamo of Bergamot and bergo-mask. The Italian city of Bergamo is situated in Lombardy, at the base of the Alps, near Lake Como and north of Milan. It is the seat of a bishop and supports silk and other textiles, together with a large trade in cattle and produce.

It has given its name to bergamot, or *Citrus bergamea*, one of the orange family, and to the orange-scented oil which is expressed or distilled from the rind of the fruit and used as a perfume.

A Bergomask was a local rustic dance and the name was also applied to a local clown or reveller.

Shakespeare, in *Midsummer Night's Dream, v. 1*, says: "Will it please you to see the epilogue, or to hear a Bergomask dance between two of our company?"

The bergamot pear is said to be named after the corruption of a Turkish term for a prince's pear.

Bethel of Bethel. Many Noncon-formist chapels are still called Bethels, which name means a hallowed spot or house of God and is derived from the place north of Jerusalem originally called Luz (*Gen. xxviii. 19*). Bethel,

the name afterwards taken by the city itself, was originally applied to a sanctuary near Luz. Jacob there had his vision of the ladder.

The name Bethesda, also applied to chapels, means a house of mercy. According to *John v. 2* "there is at Jerusalem by the sheep market a pool, which is called in the Hebrew tongue Bethesda, having five porches. In these lay a great multitude of im-potent folk, of blind, halt, withered, waiting for the moving of the water."

Bidar of Biddery ware. Biddery, or Bidri, ware, made of a characteristic metal of copper, lead, zinc and tin, derives its name from its centre of manufacture, Bidar, the town in Hyderabad, Central India, north-west of the capital city.

Big Ben of Big Ben. The time signal of the strokes of Big Ben has become a world-recognized and welcome feature of British radio transmission. Big Ben (which term is strictly applied to the great bell only, and not to the clock tower of the Houses of Parlia-ment, Westminster) takes its name, according to most accounts, from Sir Benjamin Hall. He was Chief Com-missioner of Works, 1855–8, during which term the great bell was cast for the clock tower.

It was to have been called "St. Stephen," but the random use of the name "Big Ben" in the Press immedi-ately caught the public's fancy, and has persisted.

Some claim that it was named after a popular contemporary boxer, Ben-jamin Brain, whose nickname was "Big Ben."

The first bell, cast near Stockton-on-Tees in 1856, was cracked when sounded during a week of public exhibition in Palace Yard. Two years later a second was cast at White-chapel (*q.v.*), from a design by E. B. Denison, afterwards Lord Grim-thorpe. The inscription records that it weighs 13 tons 10 cwt. 3 qrs. 15 lb. This bell was also subsequently cracked (during which period of three years the hours were sounded on a quarter bell), but then Big Ben was quarter-turned and used again for the hours.

The famous Westminster Chimes, the familiar quarter chimes, copied in many clocks, were composed by Dr. William Crotch (1775–1847), Principal of the Royal Academy of Music, 1822. It is said he re-arranged the notes of the fifth bar of Handel's famous *Messiah* aria, "I know that my Redeemer liveth." The chimes were composed for St. Mary's, Cambridge.

Billingsgate of Billingsgate. The ancient and most famous fishmarket of Billingsgate is situated near London Bridge and the Monument, on the site of a passage through the city wall which led to the wharves.

"To talk Billingsgate" or to give "Billingsgate compliments" was to imply foul, abusive language derived from the time when Billingsgate porters were noted for their uncouthness and violent vocabulary. The phrase is frequently found in literature, but is no longer fairly applicable to the market workers.

Sydney Smith (1771–1845) says: "Rather too close an imitation of that language which is used in the apostolic occupation of trafficking in fish."

A Billingsgate pheasant was at one time the term for a herring or bloater.

The Black Country. The term "The Black Country" is given to the Midland manufacturing districts of England. Birmingham is in the centre of the area, which includes Wolverhampton, Redditch, etc. The name arose from the dense clouds of smoke from the factories, from the mining activities and the general drabness of the industrial scene.

Modern methods, the advent of electricity, town planning and other improvements have done something to remove the slur of the title.

Blarney Castle of the Blarney Stone and Blarney. The town and castle of Blarney, in County Cork, Eire, is five miles north-west of the city. Its old castle, on the site of a still more ancient one built by Cormac MacCarthy, the Irish chieftain and lord of Muskerry, contains the half-ton Blarney Stone high up on the parapet of one of its thick walls. The stone is difficult of access and the daring who are able to kiss it are said to acquire the gifts of oratory and the ability to achieve their desire by cajolery or "blarney." The word has become synonymous with wheedling, seductive speech and any artifice of talk or gesture employed to gain personal ends.

The custom has attracted world travellers and any who display the qualities it is alleged to convey are described as "having kissed the Blarney Stone."

Goldsmith (1730–74) used the name Lady Blarney for one of the bright ladies in *The Vicar of Wakefield* (1766).

To blarney, in the language of the United States underworld, is to burgle, especially by picking locks.

Blenheim of Blenheim Orange, Blenheim Spaniel. Blenheim Palace, adjoining Woodstock, in Oxfordshire, was presented to the Duke of Marlborough for his victory over the French and Bavarians at Blenheim, the Bavarian village on the Danube, in 1704. It was planned by Queen Anne as a gift from the Crown, but much legislation was involved and the Duke contributed largely to the cost. He left £50,000 to finish the work and the plinth of the memorial to him in the grounds records the Act of Parliament required by the building of the so-called gift.

The architect of the Palace was Sir John Vanbrugh (1664–1726), author of *The Relapse* and other plays. His massive style, while receiving the praise of contemporary artists, including Sir Joshua Reynolds, was criticized by the wits of the day. A couplet written as epitaph ran:

*Lie heavy on him, Earth, for he
Laid many a heavy load on thee.*

It is said that the original trees, many of which remain, were laid out on a plan to represent the placing of Marlborough's men at the battle of Blenheim.

The Palace was famed for its orchards and for its orangery and the popular Blenheim Orange apple was first associated with the Palace.

The Blenheim Spaniel, which was first bred at the Palace, is one of the five varieties or strains of the King Charles Spaniel. The Duke of Marlborough used them with the gun and the strain is often depicted in the portraits of the period. Red predominates in the colouring.

The phrase "Going to Blenheim Steps" was not derived from the Palace but from the London west end site of the anatomical school organized by the famous surgeon Sir Astley Cooper (1768–1841). The expression implied that the person was going to be dissected or exhumed. Cooper's establishment was a centre of trade for the Resurrectionists, or body snatchers, and he claimed in Parliament that there was no person of any rank whom he could not dissect. The law might enhance the price, but not prevent the exhumation.

Bloomsbury of Bloomsbury. The west central district of London known as Bloomsbury lies between Gray's Inn Road and Tottenham Court Road. It includes the British Museum, the new London University buildings, University College Hospital and other public institutions. It houses many students and offers numerous hostels and hotels.

Bloomsbury was formerly a fashionable residential district, but is now regarded more as a literary, artistic and political quarter, particularly for young and unorthodox ideas, and, perhaps, seemingly out-dated ones.

The use of the word "Bloomsbury" and "Bloomsburyite" implies a faint and perhaps condescending criticism of the deliberately "out-of-step."

Bohemia of Bohemian. The ancient kingdom of Bohemia in Central Europe is now absorbed in Czechoslovakia. It was widely—but perhaps incorrectly—regarded as the country of origin of the gypsies. In consequence anyone, particularly associated with the arts, who adopted an irregular and unexpected mode of life, was dubbed Bohemian. Thackeray did much to popularize the use of the term. The adjective was also used euphemistically during the Victorian era to cover unconventionality and immorality.

Bokhara of Bokhara carpets and rugs. Bokhara, or Bukara, the capital of the former Mohammedan khanate, is now part of Soviet Turkmanistan. The New Bokhara is several miles from the ancient walled city, which was a centre of Islamic culture and commerce. It was formerly a prominent slave market. The industries include textiles, leather, cutlery, etc., and bright Bokhara carpets and rugs were an extensive export to Europe.

Bordeaux of Bordeaux. The great French city and port of south-west France is capital of the department of Gironde. It is a university city and an archiepiscopal see.

It has been famous for its red wines, of the claret type, since the 4th century. The French word *clairet* was originally applied to many light red and yellow wines to distinguish them from the usual red and white vintages. It is not there used in the sense in which it is employed in this country.

Dr. Johnson (1709–84), at a dinner with Sir Joshua Reynolds, said: "Claret is the liquor for boys; port for men; but he who aspires to be a hero must drink brandy."

Borstal of Borstal. The term Borstal has become almost synonymous with the reformation of young offenders to prevent their becoming habitual criminals.

The system, which derived to some extent from American reformatories, was started experimentally at the old convict prison at Borstal, Kent, in 1902. It was fully established by the Prevention of Crime (Borstal) Act of 1908.

Every effort is made to divert the offender's energies into properly directed and socially useful channels and the Borstal Association is responsible for after-care and the finding of employment after discharge. A high percentage of successes is recorded.

There are Borstal institutions also at Feltham and Portland and one at Aylesbury, Bucks, for female offenders.

Boston of the Boston Tea Party, Boston, etc. The capital of Massachusetts, Boston, was the scene of an act of violence on December 16, 1773, which has made the phrase "A Boston Tea Party" applicable to similar acts of irregular force, particularly in connection with politics.

A meeting of protest against dutied tea importations into the United States proved a failure and that night young men, many disguised as Indians, boarded the three British ships and threw overboard the chests of tea, so that the harbour was black with tea.

Boston, a card game which contained aspects of whist and quadrille, was said to have been invented at Boston during the late 18th century by officers of the French Fleet lying off the city. The names of two nearby islands, Great and Little Misery, correspond to terms used in the game. The game had a vogue in French society and there are many literary references to it. Some accounts claim that it was invented in Versailles and only named in honour of Boston. The game was widely popular in Europe and in America until the middle of last century.

Parthenocissus tricuspidata, known to many as Virginia creeper, is called Boston Ivy. The true and related Virginia creeper is *P. quinquefolia*.

Botany Bay of Botany Bay. The term Botany Bay, widely used in contemporary writings and still employed, less extensively, as a synonym for criminal retribution, is an inlet near Sydney, Australia. It was discovered by Captain James Cook, in 1770, and was so called by the naturalist of the party (Sir Joseph Banks, after whom the banksia is named). He was impressed by the great variety and luxuriousness of the local flora.

The place was decided upon as the site of a convict settlement at the time when chain gangs were being sent extensively to Australia (see *Tolpuddle*). The name Botany Bay became widely known, but the plans for the settlement were subsequently transferred to Sydney.

Bijayah of Bougie. The Algerian port of Bijayah, now known as Bougie, was the source of wax from which candles, tapers and similar lights were made. They are still frequently known as *bougie*, which is the French word for a candle or taper, and for a sparking plug.

A bougie in surgery (in both countries) is a thin, taper-like instrument for exploring and dilating narrow passages of the body.

Bow Bells of Within the sound of Bow Bells. To be born within the sound of Bow Bells is the general requirement of the claim to be a Cockney.

The bells referred to are not, as is frequently supposed, those of Bow, in Poplar, three miles from St. Paul's. The saying refers to the bells of St. Mary-le-Bow, Cheapside, London, E.C., a famous Wren church with a particularly notable spire, situated almost in the centre of the City. Its peal has been celebrated for centuries and in the 15th century John Dun, or Donne (a mercer, and not the poet), gave two tenements for the upkeep of Bow Bell. It was rung late in the evening to guide city travellers and later a larger bell was used to sound the end of the day's work.

The church, rebuilt after the Fire of London, was severely damaged by bombing during the Second World War.

The word Cockney, which appears to have been applied specifically to London dwellers only after the 16th century, derives from the Middle-English *coken-ey*, a "cock's egg" or the small, yolk-less egg occasionally laid by hens. The term was originally applied to a spoilt, cockered child, later by country dwellers to the then comparatively small percentage of town dwellers, and later still in its restricted sense to certain Londoners.

Cockaigne, or Cockayne, has been for centuries an imaginary land of ease and luxury. Its origin is obscure.

It has, perhaps on the basis of sound, been linked with the word cockney in its essentially London associations. Sir Edward Elgar (1857–1919) so used it in his *Cockaigne Overture*.

Bow Street of the Bow Street runners. Bow Street, which is in Covent Garden, London, running parallel with Drury Lane, is the site of the Police Court presided over by the Chief Metropolitan Magistrate. Bow Street runners, before the introduction of the Police force, scoured the country to apprehend criminals. They were commonly known as "Redbreasts" from their bright red cloth waistcoat, surmounted by a blue dress coat with brass buttons. They acted not only as detectives but as general informers and agents. Charles Dickens, in his *Letters*, recalls seeing them standing about the door of the office in Bow Street.

Bowery of the Bowery. The street in the south of New York, known as the Bowery, was formerly notorious as a hotbed of criminals and undesirable aliens. The term was used as a synonym for such classes, particularly in the United States, and gave its name also to the characteristic dialect of the neighbourhood.

Brabant of La Brabançonne. Brabant, the central, capital province of Belgium, gives its name to the country's national anthem—*La Brabançonne*. The author was a French actor named Jenneval and the composer van Campentrout (1779–1848). The Brabançons, whose spirit and courage it portrays, were in earlier centuries acclaimed as the greatest fighters in Europe.

The national anthem was written in 1830 when Brussels demonstrations achieved the separation of Belgium from Holland.

Brandenburg of the Brandenburg **Concertos.** Brandenburg is a province of Prussia. Berlin, which is in Brandenburg, is a separately governed area. The cathedral city of Brandenburg has a large textile and machinery trade, facilitated by its numerous rivers and canals in what would otherwise be a flat and barren area. The Mark of Brandenburg was united with Prussia in the 17th century and separated from Poland in the 18th century.

The six Brandenburg Concertos by J. S. Bach (1685–1750) were completed in 1721 and were dedicated to Christian Ludwig, Margrave of Brandenburg.

A Margrave was a Governor entrusted with the care of the Mark, which was not currency but the margravate, or frontier. A Margrave was immediately responsible to the king or emperor and from the 12th century the title was hereditary, acquiring in time equality with the rank of a prince of the empire.

Bray of the Vicar of Bray. The parish of Bray is near Maidenhead, in Berkshire. The origin of the vicar in the song, who trimmed his sails to whatever political wind was blowing, is said to be one Simon Eleyn, or Alleyne, Vicar of Bray and Canon of Windsor in the reign of Henry VIII. He is said, by a weathercock expediency, to have maintained his office through the reigns of Edward VI, Mary and Elizabeth.

His aim he expressed in the phrase, "Whatsoever King shall reign, still I'll be Vicar of Bray, sir."

Bridewell of Bridewell. The term Bridewell is still used as a term implying enforced correction. The original royal palace became a hospital and subsequently an institution for correction.

The palace is the scene of *Henry VIII, iii.*

The building, which was largely destroyed in the Great Fire of London, 1666, stood near the junction of the river Fleet with the Thames close to Blackfriars. The adjacent Fleet Street Wren church is dedicated to St. Bride (or Bridget).

Brie of Brie cheese. Brie, the agricultural district of Northern France, is east of Paris, bounded on the west and south by the Seine and on the north by the Marne. It is noted for dairy produce and particularly for its characteristic cream cheese.

Bristol of "Shipshape and Bristol fashion," Bristol Milk, etc. Bristol, the cathedral city and seaport of the west, is situated 6 miles from the mouth of the Avon and lies partly in Gloucestershire and partly in Somersetshire. Nearly a thousand years ago it was mentioned on coins and was then chiefly occupied with slave export. In the 14th century it was a staple town, occupied with wool, leather, etc.

Cabot sailed from Bristol on his discovery of North America in 1497.

The phrase "Shipshape and Bristol fashion" arose, according to old nautical records, as a tribute to Bristol's great commercial days of sail when the efficiency and order of the port were a byword in maritime circles.

Bristol China was made famous by Champion during the years 1773–81.

Bristol Diamonds was the name given to certain colourless crystal quartz found near Clifton, Bristol.

The Bristol Boy was the title applied to Thomas Chatterton (1752–70), who was born in the City and wrote there his *Poems*, purporting to be the work of an imaginary Bristol poet of the 15th century, Thomas Rowley.

To-day the vast Corporation-owned Docks handle an extensive trade in West Indies produce, petroleum, tobacco, etc.

Bristol Milk and Bristol Cream are noted brands of sherry supplied by John Harvey & Sons, Ltd., since their foundation in 1796. At one time Sherry Sack, called Bristol Milk, was given by Bristol residents to their friends and became particularly associated with the City and named after it. Thomas Fuller (1608–91), in his *Worthies of England*, writes: "This metaphorical milk, whereby Xeres or Sherry-sack is intended." Samuel Pepys (1633–1703), in his *Diary*, under the date 13th June, 1668, says: "How they did give us good entertainment of strawberries, a whole venison pasty, cold and plenty of brave wine, and above all Bristol Milk."

Daniel Defoe (1660–1731) records that in Bristol's taverns "Bristol Milk, which is Spanish sherry nowhere so good as here, is plentifully drunk."

Bristol Cream Sherry appeared much later; at the beginning of the present century. At that time the House of Harvey was shipping a nameless rich full pale sherry and when it was served to King Edward VII on one of his visits to the City, he remarked: "If that is Bristol Milk this should be Bristol Cream."

Bristol Board, used by artists and draughtsmen, properly consists of several layers of fine rag paper pressed together, but wood pulp and esparto are now used for some products so named.

Broadmoor of Broadmoor. The State criminal mental hospital is situated in Berkshire, near Crowthorne. It was built in 1863.

Birmingham of Brummagem. The great midland city of Birmingham, which is the centre of the hardware trade and a vast industrial area concerned also with heavy engineering, chemicals, etc., is a university and cathedral city.

In former times it was regarded as a world factory and mart for cheap toys, tawdry jewellery, imitation stones, plated goods, etc. Counterfeit groats were at one time made in the city.

Much of the material was shoddy, and, in consequence, the local corruption of the City's name (still noted in "The Brums," applied to the football team) was given to much tawdry and superficially attractive material, irrespective of its place of origin. It implied a certain critical contempt.

Brussels of Brussels carpets, sprouts. Brussels, the Brabant capital of Belgium, is the centre of administration, education and art. It is famous for its historic buildings and beautiful architecture. Its industries include textiles, Brussels lace, and the noted carpets, a combination of linen and worsted, with the latter revealing the pattern. The carpets were brought to Kidderminster (*q.v.*) in the 18th century.

Brussels sprouts, a popular green vegetable whose associations with the city are remote, are a variety of *Brassica* forming leaf-buds, like minute cabbages, in the axils of the leaves on the main stem.

Bengal of Bungalow, Bengal stripes, etc. The province of Bengal, India, through the Hindu word *bangla* meaning Bengalese, is responsible for the word bungalow. It was originally applied to a one-storeyed house with a verandah, a type of residence used extensively by Europeans in India. Nowadays, in Britain and America, the word has a wider range and tends to include any type of lightly erected houses, particularly for holiday and seaside use.

The name Bengal is also found in Bengal stripes, a specific pattern of gingham (Mal. *ginggang*—striped) which originated in the province. Bengal hemp, when its leaves are dried, produces *bhang*, which is smoked with or without tobacco and *hashish*, which latter narcotic is also made from other hemps.

It is thought that the word *assassin* derives from *hashshin*, the Arabic for hemp-eaters, owing to the violence frequently committed when under the influence of the *hashish* taken in excess.

Bengal lights are vivid blue lights used as distress signals at sea. The Bengal tiger is the true or royal tiger.

Buncombe of Bunkum. Buncombe is a county in North Carolina, U.S.A. In 1820 its representative in Congress made an ornate, irrelevant and frequently interrupted speech. When challenged he replied that he was not speaking to the Congress so much as to Buncombe—to his constituents who expected it. The word bunkum was immediately applied to any political claptrap or vote-catching device and extended to cover any dubious and suspected statement.

Burgundy of Burgundy, Burgonet. The French province of Burgundy, comprises four departments, is world famous for its wines, including Chambertin and Clos Vougeot (red), and Chablis (white). Many of the famous vineyards are on the slopes of the

Côte-d'Or. Dijon (the ancient capital), Beaune and Mâcon (which two last-named towns are made famous by local wines) are among the chief centres of Burgundy.

The burgonet, a closely fitting visored helmet, derives its name from the old French name for Burgundy, with which country it was originally associated.

This day I'll wear aloft my burgonet—
As on a mountain-top the cedar shows,
That keeps his leaves in spite of any storm . . .
Warwick, in *2 Henry VI, v. 1.*

Burlington House of Burlington House. The Piccadilly home of the Royal Academy in Burlington House has caused the name to be almost synonymous. The House, which was begun by the first Earl of Burlington in the 17th century, in fact now houses several other learned societies. It was purchased by the State in 1854. (See *Savile Row.*)

Burslem of Burslem ware. In the 17th century the Staffordshire town of Burslem was the centre of the English pottery industry and is still frequently referred to as "The Mother of the Potteries."

It was the birthplace of Joseph Wedgwood (1730–95).

Before the 18th century English pottery was of little account and most common china was obtained from Holland and fine porcelain from China.

Wedgwood revolutionized the industry which had already been started in Burslem by some Dutch potters.

Wedgwood's production of earthenware and white stone ware established British Pottery and made Burslem ware famous.

The Potteries were a favourite subject in the novels of Arnold Bennett (1867–1931). His "Five Towns," presented in several books are, under assumed names, Burslem, Tunstall, Hanley, Stoke-on-Trent and Longton.

Byzantium of Byzantine. Constantinople, captured by the Turks in the 15th century, was formerly known as Byzantium. For many centuries previously Byzantine art and architecture had been famous. Its distinguishing features, the round arch, cross, circle, dome, etc., with lavish use of mosaic work, are notably seen in St. Mark's, Venice, and are copied in many modern buildings.

Caerphilly of Caerphilly cheese. The Glamorgan town of Caerphilly, a few miles from Cardiff, produced and gave its name to what has probably been the most famous Welsh cheese for four centuries, *Caws Caerffili.*

The first Caerphilly Market was an open one into which were brought the round flat cheeses from far afield. During the latter half of the 19th century, the old market was replaced by a roofed building. Sale of the cheese reached its zenith towards the end of last century, and as much as 2½ tons were disposed of weekly. In 1910 the Highbridge, Somerset, market was opened for the sale of the cheese and the Caerphilly market closed down. Large quantities of the cheese are still made by the farmers of Monmouthshire and Glamorgan, and its fame persists.

Cairngorm of Cairngorm Stone (Cairngorum). The Cairngorm peak and district of the Grampian range, in Banffshire, Scotland, was the place of discovery of the cairngorm, or Cairngorm stone.

The mineral occurs in crystals of quartz running through the coarse granite. It reveals grey to brown colourings, induced by an organic content.

It is very popular in Scotland for ornamental purposes and finds its place in characteristic brooches, pins, bracelets, dirk handles, etc.

Calcutta of the Black Hole of Calcutta, Calcutta Sweepstake. The notorious event which placed the name of the great Indian city in a phrase of still current usage occurred in 1756. Then the town was sacked by Suraj-ud-Dowlah, the Nawab of Bengal. The Englishmen, who were forced to surrender, were driven into a small ill-ventilated guard chamber. After a night of intense heat only 23 of the 146 prisoners were alive.

The phrase is used to describe any notoriously inadequate or insanitary accommodation.

The great city is also known to millions throughout the world by its famous Sweepstake. It is run on the result of the English Derby and is organized by the Royal Calcutta Turf Club. Although it is nominally private and confined to members, tickets do in fact find their way all over the world. The prizes amount to many thousands of pounds.

Calicut of Calico. Calicut is a seaport in the Malabar district of India, on the south-eastern seaboard. It was the first place in India to be visited by Europeans and was then a great centre of native trade, particularly in cotton spinning and weaving. Calico, to which the port gave its name, is still a prominent export, though the cotton material is also made elsewhere, including the British Isles.

California of the Californian Redwood or Sequoia. Films and travel books have made the Californian Redwoods the symbol of nature's supreme magnificence in the world of trees.

The redwoods (*S. sempervirens*), which predominate in the Californian foothills, achieve great heights and present a magnificent appearance. The bark yields fibre and offers fire resistance. The timber is valuable. The needle-like foliage of the conifer resembles that of the Yew. It propagates freely and heights of over 300 ft. and girths of 70 ft. are on record.

The Big Tree, another Sequoia (*Gigantea*), is also known as the Wellingtonia, Washingtonia, or Mammoth Tree. Its scale-like foliage distinguishes it from the Redwood. It flourishes in the Sierra Nevada district of California and though it propagates freely is subject to Government protection. It reaches heights of well over 300 ft.

Both varieties have been introduced with some success to Great Britain, but the trees have not reached such magnificent heights.

The Californian Incense Cedar, characterized by the clothing of its erect trunk in dark green foliage, is found also in many parts of the Pacific zone. It is planted in limited numbers in Britain, mainly for ornamental purposes. The tree has a plume-like contour, similar to that of the Lombardy poplar (*q.v.*), but with a coniferous density and without the characteristic quivering of the poplar leaves.

Calvary of Calvary. The word Calvary is a Latin translation of the Greek *golgotha*, a skull. Golgotha, "the place of a skull," was the site of Christ's crucifixion (*Matt. xxvii. 33*). The name is thought to have arisen through a resemblance to a skull in the formation of the land. Mount Calvary is north-west of the city of Jerusalem.

The term calvary is now applied to a crucifix and to any representation of the scene. It is also, in a personal sense, applied to the final agony of a person or even of a movement.

Camberwell of the Camberwell Beauty. Camberwell is a Parliamentary and metropolitan borough, south-east of London. The beautiful butterfly, *Vanessa antiopa*, common in south and east Europe and North America, was found occasionally and noted in Camberwell when the district was a rural area.

Cambrai of Cambric. Cambrai, the ancient cathedral town of France, in the Department du Nord, near the Belgian frontier, still includes among its manufactures cambric which was named after the town. It is a fine white linen now also manufactured elsewhere. Two great battles took place round Cambrai in the First World War.

The material is mentioned in *The Winter's Tale, iv. 3.*

Camembert of Camembert cheese. The little Normandy town of Camembert, world famous for its cheese, came into prominence in this connection in the 18th century when Mme Marie Harel, at the age of twenty-five, discovered the formula in 1786. In ten years the cheese was famous. The inventor's grave, with a statue, is at Vimoutiers, 2 miles from Camembert, and it is honoured at each annual fair.

The soft, rennet cheese is ripened for several weeks before marketing and at its best should be almost fluid in consistency.

Canaan of Canaan, a land of promise. The Old Testament name for Palestine was Canaan, after Canaan, the fourth son of Ham (*Gen. x. 6, ix. 22–7*).

It was the Promised Land offered to Abraham for his obedience (*Exod. xii. 25*), the land "flowing with milk and honey" (*Exod. iii. 8*). The name is now used to denote any place of great promise and prosperity.

Canary Islands of Canaries, Canary bananas, Canary sack, etc. The group of thirteen volcanic islands known as the Canaries is situated in the Atlantic, off the north-west coast of Africa. It forms a province of Spain. The seven major islands are Grand Canary, Teneriffe, Palma, Ferro or Hierro, Lanzarote, Gomera and Fuerteventura. They are very rugged islands, with peaks rising in Teneriffe to over 12,000 ft. There is a large trade in tropical produce and the healthy climate, with little summer rain, encourages tourist centres and health resorts.

The name Canary is thought to derive from the Latin, *canis*, a dog, as the islands were recorded in Roman times as possessing large dogs.

Canaries, or Canary finches, are plentiful in these islands and in Madeira and the Azores. In the wild state the birds are greenish with brown streaks. The typical Canary yellow, which gives its name to the general colour, is the result of breeding. East Anglia, and particularly Norwich, is a centre of canary breeding and exhibition. There is much cross-breeding of the birds in the Tyrol.

The islands have given their name to many products once or still raised extensively there: bananas, seed of the Canary grass, *Phalaris canariensis*, etc.

Canary sack (the word comes from the French *sec*, meaning dry) was popular in Tudor times and is still a favourite wine.

Falstaff, in *I Henry IV, ii. 4*, says: "If sack and sugar be a fault, God help the wicked!"

Malvoisie, otherwise Malvasia or Malmsey, is a sweet, fortified wine made from white grapes. It takes its name from Malvasia, in the Morea, which is connected with Greece by the isthmus of Corinth.

The wines were introduced to the Canaries and Madeira five hundred years ago.

History records that by the order of Richard III, his brother, the Duke of Clarence, was drowned in a butt of Malmsey in the 15th century.

The famous vineyards in Palma, producing Malvoisie, Malvasia and Malmsey, suffered disastrous damage by volcanic eruption in 1949.

The Canary which Shakespeare mentions in *All's Well that Ends Well, II, i*, and elsewhere, is an old dance, similar to a gigue. It is associated with the Canary Islands but is thought to be of Spanish origin, where it was danced with castanets.

Cantaloupe Castle of Cantaloupes. The small, round musk melons, ribbed and with a characteristic meshed surface, are known as Cantaloupes from their original association with Cantaloupe Castle of Ancona, the city and province of Italy.

It is one of the four provinces of the Marches compartimento and sustains a large trade in wines, produce, silk and other textiles. It is an important port and railway centre on the Adriatic in central Italy.

Before the middle of the 19th century Ancona was included in Papal territory.

Canterbury of Canterbury Bells. The Kentish cathedral city of Canterbury, on the Stour, is the seat of the primate and the ecclesiastical metropolis of Britain. The see was founded by St. Augustine in the 6th century and, in addition to its founder, is famous for its association with such great holders of the archiepiscopal office as St. Dunstan, Thomas à Becket (who was murdered in the Cathedral), Cranmer and Laud.

The Archbishop of Canterbury is first peer of the realm and crowns the sovereign in Westminster Abbey.

Canterbury is of great historic interest, is the centre of much of the county's trade in hops, fruit, etc., and still maintains a weaving industry introduced by the Huguenots. It has many literary associations, and the ancient King's school is famous.

The association of the flower, Canterbury Bell (*Campanula medium*), is said to derive from the bell-shaped tokens and amulets purchased and worn by pilgrims to Canterbury in early days.

The name *Campanula* is a diminutive of the latin *Campana*, a bell, and the species, which is native to Central Europe, is also known as the Coventry bell.

Chaucer's pilgrims set out for Canterbury from the Tabard Inn, Southwark, London.

At one time the phrase "A Canterbury story" was used as a synonym for a romantic yarn or far-fetched tale, from association with the *Canterbury*

Tales. The great work, which is incomplete in that there are no narratives for the journey home, was written about 1387.

The phrase "Canterbury's the higher rack, but Winchester's the better manger," is attributed to a 14th-century Bishop of Winchester who was offered the archbishopric. It referred to the then higher income of the see of Winchester.

Weaving has been carried on in Canterbury since Huguenot days, and since the Second World War the Canterbury weavers have done much to spread the revival of the craft in Britain.

Capri of Capri. The beautiful island of Capri, at the south of the Bay of Naples, possesses a cathedral city in its capital. The island is only 9 miles in circumference and the other town is Anacapri, north of which is the famous Blue Grotto. The chief products of the island are fruit, oil and wine. The latter, known as Capri, is made in two qualities, white and red. The adjoining mainland province of Campagna produces many wines, including the well-known, straw-coloured Lacrima Christi del Vesuvio, product of grapes grown on the southern slopes of Mount Vesuvius.

Capri has been the residence of many writers and artists and has become particularly associated in recent years with Dr. Axel Munthe's *The Story of San Michele* (1929).

Cardigan of Cardigan. The name cardigan, for the popular knitted over-waistcoat, derives from the South Wales county, through its 7th Earl (1797–1868). He popularized the garment which then largely superseded the waistcoat. He was born in Hambledon, Hants, and led the famous Charge of the Light Brigade at Balaclava in 1854.

Carey Street of Carey Street. The Lincoln's Inn street which runs between Chancery Lane and Portugal Street, London, is synonymous, in popular expression, with bankruptcy. This is due to the location there of the Bankruptcy Buildings which house the offices of the Department of the Official Assignee, the Official Receiver in Bankruptcy, the Companies' Court, Registrar's Office, and the High Court of Justice in Bankruptcy.

Mount Carmel of Carmelite. Mount Carmel is a range of mountains, some 20 miles in length, on the coast of Palestine near Haifa and Acre (Akka). In Biblical times it was in the province of Phœnicia, with the ports of Tyre and Sidon to the north and Nazareth to the south-east.

The Carmelites, or Friars of the Order of our Lady of Mount Carmel, have been established there since the 12th century and many authorities claim that Mount Carmel was occupied from the time of Elijah by anchorites who were subsequently converted to Christianity.

The Mount is particularly associated with the prophet who there slew the prophets of Baal (*1 Kings xviii*), restored the Shunamite's son to life (*2 Kings iv. 25–37*), and gathered all the children of Israel to decide whether Baal or Jehovah was the true God (*1 Kings xviii*).

The Carmelites, who wear a grey habit, are known as the White Friars. They were at first hermits, but in the 13th century the Order became one of mendicant friars. They sustain many houses in Britain and the name persists in White Friars and Carmelite Street in the Temple district, between Fleet Street and the Thames, which was formerly an establishment of the Order.

To-day Mount Carmel is also known as Jebel Kurmul.

Caryæ of Caryatid. The town in Laconia named Caryæ was famous for its maidens and the name caryatid is given to the female figures frequently used to support a pillar or column.

Originally caryatids were used instead of columns to support the entablature of the temples. Now the figures are more frequently used as decorations than as supports.

Male figures similarly used were known at Atlantes.

Kashmir of Cashmere. The silky woollen fabric known as cashmere was first manufactured from the hair of the Tibetan and Bokhara goats, which have since been introduced with varying success into other countries. The small goats are noted for their long, fine hair which was spun by women and woven into shawls, etc., at Cashmere, or Kashmir, the northern Indian State, adjoining Tibet. The capital is Srinagar.

Kerseymere, a twilled woollen cloth, is said by some to be corruptively named after Cashmere; by others to derive from the man's name of Casimir.

Kersey, a coarse, "honest" cloth, derives its name from Kersey, the lovely Suffolk village which lies across the river Brett, where it originated. The woollen cloth has a smooth, soft surface with a diagonally ribbed pattern. The name, used in adjectival sense to imply homely honesty, is to be found in *Love's Labour's Lost, v. 2.*

Catawba of Catawba grape and wine. The river Catawba of the Carolinas, on the eastern seaboard of the United States, is said to be the original place of cultivation of the Catawba sweet, red fox grape, *Vitis Labrusca,* which is used extensively in the manufacture of still and sparkling wine.

Cayenne of Cayenne pepper. The port of Cayenne is the capital of French Guiana, on the north coast of South America. It trades in gold and tropical produce.

Cayenne, or red pepper, much used in pickles, flavourings, etc., is ground from the pods and seeds of the Capsicum which, in most of its strains, yields pepper of differing types. *C. longum* is known as the Chili.

Chablis of Chablis. The small French town of Chablis, noted for its white wine, particularly commended for consumption with oysters, is situated in the Yonne department of France. It is a few miles from the capital, Auxerre, and just over 100 miles south-east of Paris.

Champagne of Champagne. Champagne, from which the name of the wine was first taken, is a district of France lying to the east and north-east of Paris. It includes Rheims and its northern border adjoins Belgium. The land is chiefly flat, particularly fertile in the west, and its vineyards produce the famous champagne. It appears to have made its first recorded appearance in the late 14th century when Charles IV of France welcomed King Wenceslaus of Bohemia at Rheims.

Champagne is made chiefly from black grapes and the juice is run away from the skins, which contain the colouring matter.

A blend is known as a cuvee, and shippers make up their own brands. Some cuvees may consist of blends of different vintages.

Champagne did not originally sparkle and effervesce. The discovery of these now characteristic qualities is attributed by the industry to a blind Benedictine monk, named Perignon, of the 17th/18th century. Containers of the wine had previously been stopped with porous wood and the monk, convinced that valuable gases and properties thereby escaped, experimented over years with different materials for stoppers. Then a traveller gave him a piece of Spanish cork and he had found the solution, though he did not live long enough to see the full fruits of his patient research and discovery in the local industry.

The French courts decided early this century that the name Champagne could no longer be regarded as applicable only to the products of the Champagne district.

Charleston of the Charleston. The American dance known as the Charleston, characterized by side-kicks from the knee, takes its name from Charleston, the port and capital city of South Carolina on the eastern seaboard of the United States. It has a large commerce in cotton, rice and phosphates.

The city is the seat of a Roman Catholic bishop.

Chartreuse of Chartreuse, Carthusian, Charterhouse. La Grande Chartreuse, a monastery founded by St. Bruno in the 11th century, was situated 12 miles north of Grenoble, in the south-east of France. Its name derived from a near village of Cartusia.

St. Hugh of Lincoln was a Carthusian monk who came to England in the 12th century and the Order was established in many countries.

The monks were evicted by the French government at the beginning of this century. They were famous for the manufacture of the liqueur, chartreuse, made from brandy and aromatic herbs. They were in exile at Tarragonne, Spain, until 1929, when they returned to France, and in 1940 reoccupied their old monastery.

The famous public school, The Charterhouse, was in its original London site built upon the site of what had been a Carthusian monastery until 1535. Its scholars are known as Carthusians.

It was purchased from the Earl of Suffolk in 1611 as a home for aged men, the "Brothers of Charterhouse." The School removed to Godalming, Surrey, in 1872. Charterhouse, as the Greyfriars School, is described in detail in *The Newcombes*, by Thackeray (1811–63). He was educated at Charterhouse.

Cheddar of Cheddar cheese. The noted English cheese takes its name from the Somerset town of Cheddar, 20 miles from Bristol and 8 from Wells. In addition to the extensive cheese manufacture in the district, the town is noted for the famous Cheddar Gorge, the rocky approach from the Mendips, for the large stalactite caves and for remains of Roman settlements.

Cheddar cheese is manufactured extensively in the United States and marketed under many names.

Chelsea of Chelsea Pensioners. The South-West London borough of Chelsea has many historic, art and literary associations, but is chiefly connected in the public's mind with the Chelsea Pensioners, whose distinctive scarlet, bemedalled uniforms are a feature of the capital.

The pensioners are inmates of the Chelsea Royal Hospital, founded by Charles II in 1682 at the instance—accounts, perhaps romantically, claim —of Nell Gwynne. It was built by Wren and opened in 1694. It accommodates over 500 In-Pensioners, old and disabled soldiers. Trophies are to be seen in the Great Hall, which is open to the public, as are the extensive grounds. They include the former gardens of Ranelagh.

The borough was formerly famous for porcelain and bun shops. The latter were patronized by Londoners from all parts. Congreve (1670–1729) refers to it in *Love for Love, II. ii.*

The Chelsea bun is a wound strip, generally containing currants and often sugared or iced.

Chesapeake Bay of Chesapeake Bay or American Duck Retriever. Chesapeake Bay, the vast inlet on the east coast of the United States of America, divides Maryland and forms the eastern boundary of Virginia. Many great rivers, including the Susquehanna and the Potomac, flow into it.

It was the breeding ground of the original Chesapeake Retrievers, the red or tan sporting dogs that have a passion for water and are fitted thereto by possessing webbed feet and an unusually thick undercoat which is waterproof.

The breed is thought to have originated at the opening of the 19th century and to have arisen through a cross of Otterhounds and Newfoundland dogs introduced by the survivors of an English wreck off the coast of the bay.

The breed is now popular in many countries and possesses almost unrivalled qualities for water work.

Cheshire of Cheshire cheese, etc.

Cheshire, the north-west county bounded on the north by the Irish Sea, has given its name to the characteristic locally made and famous cheese.

Cheshire is perhaps the strongest claimant to the honour of being the first county to introduce organized horse racing in the British Isles, dating from the early 16th century. A happy custom since 1894 has been the presentation of prime Cheshire cheeses to the owners of the first three horses in the Chester Cup. The race was instituted in 1824.

The phrase "To grin like a Cheshire cat" is still used for people with a wide mouth and vacuous expression, but association with the county has never been satisfactorily explained. Some authorities assert that originally Cheshire cheeses were frequently moulded in the design of a grinning cat's face.

Lewis Carroll introduces the Cheshire cat in this association in *Alice in Wonderland*, 1869.

The Cheshire Cheese, a famous Fleet Street hostelry, has many literary associations, notably the patronage of Dr. Samuel Johnson (1709–84).

The Cheviots of Cheviot wool and cloth.

The Cheviots, the Border range of hills between England and Scotland, are partly volcanic in origin but support notable pasture land. From the sheep raised thereon are produced wool and cloths made therefrom which take the name of the district.

The Cheviot (2,700 ft.) is the chief peak of the range, which runs south-west to north-east between Northumberland and Roxburgh.

Chevy Chase of to chevy or chivy.

The verb "to chevy" (or "chivy"), meaning to scamper, chase, or, less correctly but more generally, to hustle, prod and mildly stampede, derives from *The Ballad of Chevy Chase*, mentioned in Percy's *Reliques* (1765). It probably dates from the 15th century.

It referred if not to the name of an actual house, at least to an actual chase which took place between the incessantly conflicting Border families of Percy and Douglas. In the *Ballad* the two parties meet and fight to the death and it refers to the chase of the Douglas among the "Chyviat hills" after Percy, Earl of Northumberland, had boasted that he would hunt for three days on his rival's territory without asking permission.

The skirmish is not thought to have been the Battle of Otterburn, as cited in some accounts.

Chianti of Chianti.

The popular, modestly priced Italian wine, Chianti, is associated all over the world with its decorative wicker flask, a Tuscan invention. It takes its name from the Chianti, a group of mountains near Siena, in Tuscany; due south of Florence. The mountain slopes are devoted to noted vineyards, olive groves and mulberry plantations.

Chianti is a dry, red wine, often slightly prickly when young.

Brolio, another Tuscan red wine, is named from the Castello di Brolio, in Chianti.

Chile of the Chile Pine, or "Monkey Puzzle."

The most unusual and most noticed tree in Great Britain is the Chile Pine or "Monkey Puzzle."

It is a native of southern Chile, and there are extensive forests of the tree in the province of Arauco (*q.v.*); hence its botanical name, *Araucaria araucana*. In its native habitat the seeds are eaten as food.

The species was first discovered by a Spaniard in 1780 but its introduction to Europe is credited to a British botanist, Archibald Menzies, who accompanied the British navigator, George Vancouver, on his expeditions in the late 18th century.

The broad, pointed triangular leaves are like scales and completely conceal the branches. They are dark green, almost black, and the tree's appearance is exotic and almost "surrealist." The popular name is an acknowledgment of the claim that even a monkey could not negotiate the Chile pine's sharp perils.

The Chilterns of the Chiltern Hundreds. The Chilterns are a range of chalk hills running through parts of Oxfordshire, Buckinghamshire, Bedfordshire and Hertfordshire. They rise to a height of 885 ft. near Wendover, Bucks.

A Member of Parliament applies for the Stewardship of the Chiltern Hundreds when he wishes to resign his seat. An old English Statute required that no member could vacate his seat and when this rule was amended in 1707 it provided that members could resign provided they held an office of profit from the Crown. Among such offices were eight crown stewardships whose holders were not exempt from Parliamentary duties. In 1750 a member for Wareham wished to resign his seat in order to stand at Dorchester. He sought the office of Steward of the Chiltern Hundreds, secured it and stood for his new constituency.

The Hundred was a name given to mediæval English law courts, concerned with lesser crimes, tax and road administration, etc. There were six Hundreds and Escheatorships in other parts of Britain: Berks.; Hempholme, Yorks.; Old Shoreham, Sussex; Poynings, Sussex; and Escheators of Ulster and Munster.

The Chiltern Hundreds were made up of three ancient divisions in the Chilterns; Stoke, Burnham and Desborough. The revenue of such Stewardships was once appreciable but is now nominal, as are the duties. The post can be resigned when the former member seeks re-election.

In addition to the Chiltern Hundreds, the Stewardship of the Manor of Northstead in Yorkshire also survives and the office could be similarly sought to secure retirement from the Lower House. The gift of both is in the hands of the Chancellor of the Exchequer.

The Escheatorships in Ireland were claimed for the same purpose, up to 1820 in the case of Munster and 1819 in the case of Ulster.

China of China, China tea, clay, Chow-Chow, etc. The vast Chinese republic claims a civilization of great antiquity and a culture in which all the arts flowered. Porcelain, the finer qualities of china, was first brought to Europe from China.

China tea was one of the chief exports until the competition of Indian and Ceylon varieties. Tea plantations flourish in the southern and western provinces.

The southern regions support semitropical produce and the China orange was the source of this fruit (see "All Lombard Street to a China orange").

China Clay, or Kaolin, derives its name from the Chinese Kao-ling hills, the centre of the porcelain industry. It is mined extensively in Cornwall. It is a very fine white powdered form of hydrated aluminium silicate. Kaolin, which is extensively exported, is used in the manufacture of quality paper, in porcelain manufacture and for medicines and cosmetics. Since the Second World War, by-products have been used for building construction.

Galls from China are used in the production of Chinese ink.

Chinese grass, or Boehmeria, has long, tough bast fibres which are woven into cloth and mats, etc. The plant is a native of China and Japan.

Chinese lanterns are a feature of many Chinese festivals in which ingenious paper contrivances are extensively employed for decorative purposes.

Chinese crackers are used on similar occasions.

Cathay, the name frequently found in literature, was that of China under the Mongol dynasty, the Khitans.

> To eat the lotus of the Nile
> and drink the poppies of Cathay.
>
> Whittier (1807–92).

The dog correctly called the Chow Chow, but more generally Chow, was known and bred in China for many centuries before it was acclimatized elsewhere. It was bred primarily for eating and for its pelts; the latter made attractive by the fine, long hair. It is still so bred in parts of China and Mongolia.

The Chow Chow achieved substantial recognition in Britain about fifty years ago, when the Chow Chow club was formed. The breed is instantly recognized by its black tongue and striking ruffle.

The name Chow is a corruption and is slang for China or Chinese in several countries.

Chow Chow is also a preserve consisting of orange and other fruit peels, ginger, etc.; and the name given to a vegetable pickle with a mustard sauce and spices.

Christiania (Oslo) of Christie. The expert swing in skiing, used to stop abruptly, is named after Christiania and abbreviated to Christie. The capital of Norway changed its name on January 1, 1925, replacing the Danish name with that of the ancient city of Oslo, long since obliterated, whose charter dated from the 11th century. (See *Telemark*.)

Cilicia of Cilice, Cilicious. The Asia Minor province of Cilicia, whose capital was Tarsus, gave its name to the hair-cloth garment and to the adjective, cilicious, meaning made of hair-cloth. It is in the south of Turkey, with a Mediterranean seaboard north of Cyprus.

Tarsus is particularly associated with St. Paul, who was born there and returned to the city frequently. "Afterwards I came into the regions of Syria and Cilicia" (*Gal. i. 21*).

The sackcloth of the Bible was made of goat's hair, which was also used in the making of sacks. The material was worn by mourners (*Gen. xxxvii. 34, etc.*) and as a symbol of penitence (*Matt. xi. 21*).

Calabria of Ciro di Calabria. The southernmost province of Italy, Calabria, adjoining Sicily, gives its name to the red wine, Ciro di Calabria, which comes from the province of Catanzaro. The capital is a cathedral city and the wine, olives and fruit are cultivated.

Other wines of Calabria are Savuto, from Cosenza, and Greco di Gerace, named from the east coast port.

Citeaux of Cistercian. The Cistercian Order, founded in the 11th century, takes its name from Cîteaux, near Dijon, Côte d'Or, France, where the first monastery was established by a Benedictine abbot. St. Bernard joined the Order in the 12th century. Clairvaux later became the centre of the movement, which spread rapidly in many countries, including Britain and the United States. The Cistercians, who wear a white habit, include the Trappists, named later from their abbey of La Trappe. They maintain a rule of silence.

The first Trappists reached Baltimore in 1805.

The Clyde of Clydesdale horses and terriers. The heavy draught horses known as Clydesdales were originally bred in the Clyde area of Scotland.

There is also a Clydesdale or Paisley terrier, which resembles the Skye terrier and has been recognized as a distinct breed since the beginning of this century.

Colchester of Colchester Natives. Colchester, the largest town in Essex, is built upon the site of the ancient Roman walled town of Camalodunumis on the right bank of the Colne.

It is world famous for its oyster beds and Colchester natives are cited throughout world markets. The opening of the oyster season, in September, is the occasion for ancient traditional ceremony.

The Mayor, accompanied by the Town Clerk, makes the season's first dredge in Pyfleet Creek. Yachts in the harbour are generally dressed overall and an ancient proclamation is read which records that the fisheries in the River Colne "from time beyond which memory runneth not to the contrary belonged and appertains to the corporation of the borough of Colchester."

At the following luncheon, at which prices are fixed, the loyal toast is drunk in glasses of gin.

Sprats, which are caught locally, were once referred to as the "weavers' beef of Colchester."

Colchis of Colchicum. The ancient country at the east end of the Black Sea was the home of the meadow-saffron, or colchicum. The country was prominent in Greek mythology as the destination of the Argonauts. Medea, the enchantress daughter of Æetes, king of Colchis, lived there and the territory was associated with the fount of sorcery.

Colchicum, the meadow saffron or autumn crocus, is one of several species which flourish in many countries. A characteristic of it is that when its flower appears in autumn, without leaves, the ovary remains below ground to ensure protection from cold. Fertilization is by bees and insects. The foliage appears in the spring. The corm, of small nut size, has an acrid taste which disappears when the corm is dried. The drug colchicum can be extracted from corm or seeds and is employed extensively in medicine.

It is used in the treatment of rheumatism, gout, etc., and acts as a diuretic and laxative. Taken in excess it is poisonous.

The word colchis can be seen in several plant names. The bladder nut, for instance, which came from the Caucasus, is the *Staphylea colchica*.

Coldstream of the Coldstream Guards. Coldstream, formerly called Lennel or Leinhall, is a borough in Berwickshire, on the Tweed, 14 miles from Berwick and 50 from Edinburgh.

The Coldstream Guards, the second oldest regiment in the British Army, is one of the foot guard regiments in the Household Brigade.

It was founded in 1659 by General Monk, whose name the regiment first received. The Guards marched from Coldstream in January, 1660, with the intention of bringing Charles II back to the throne. The army numbered about 6,000 men. Under their new title they then became part of the King's Household Brigade.

Coldstream for some centuries shared with Gretna Green the distinction of being a haven for eloping couples who could be married there without licence or minister.

Colney Hatch of Colney Hatch. The district of Colney Hatch, once a Middlesex hamlet and now absorbed in Greater London, is near New Southgate, London, N. It was the site chosen for the vast London County Council Asylum and as such the name became synonymous with lunacy; "He should be in Colney Hatch," etc. In 1903 a disastrous fire in the Jewish wing involved much loss of life.

Cologne of eau-de-Cologne. The

great fortified city of Cologne, on the Prussian Rhine, is one of Germany's chief commercial centres. As such it was severely devastated during the Second World War. It is a great port, the seat of an archbishop and noted for its University.

The famous perfume, eau-de-Cologne, is thought to have been invented by Johann Maria Farina (1685–1766), but subsequently the original recipe was claimed by many of the numerous firms manufacturing this valuable export. Farina came to Cologne as a youth from Northern Italy.

The perfume and restorative is made from distilled alcohol and several essential aromatic oils, including Bergamot (*q.v.*).

The *Cologne Post* was a famous newspaper issued under great mechanical and distributive difficulties by British Army officers during the British Occupation after the First World War.

Cologne, until vast rebuilding and sanitary schemes at the end of the 19th century, was notorious for narrow, smelly streets. This picture of the city is vividly presented by Samuel Taylor Coleridge (1772–1834) in his poem named after the City:

In Koln, a town of monks and bones,
And pavements fanged with murderous stones,
And rags, and hags, and hideous wenches:
I counted two and seventy stenches,
All well defined, and several stinks!
Ye Nymphs that reign o'er sewers and sinks,
The river Rhine, it is well known,
Doth wash your city of Cologne;
But tell me, Nymphs! what power divine
Shall henceforth wash the river Rhine?

Eau-de-Nil is a greenish colour so named because it is supposed to resemble the colour of the waters of the Nile.

Colophon of Colophon. The colophon, a publisher's individual mark or ornament, is said by some authorities to derive from the Greek word for "summit," and by others to have taken its name from the town of Colophon, in Lydia, Asia Minor. There the local cavalry was noted for giving the finishing touch to conflicts and the colophon originally was the finishing touch, or tail-piece, in books. It was often ornamental and accompanied by relative information.

It has now been transferred to the title page and formalized into a sign or symbol which may be used in many other ways—on the spines of books, notepaper, hanging signs, advertising, vans, etc.—as the publisher's distinguishing mark or imprint. Many colophons are historic in literature and noted artists have been employed in the devising of them.

Colophony, a distilled dark resin, is generally agreed to have derived its name from the same Lydia, town of its source and association.

Colorado of Colorado beetle. A century ago the potato crops of vast areas of the United States of America, and particularly those of the west central state of Colorado, were destroyed by a small beetle of the *Chrysomelidæ* family. The small, brightly striped insect, which feeds on vegetables, was thereafter popularly—or unpopularly—known as the Colorado beetle. Its ravages are still extensive and difficult to resist and stringent regulations for its control are statutory in many countries, including Great Britain.

Cyprus of Copper. The large Mediterranean island of Cyprus is responsible, through the latin *Cyprium*, for the word copper. It was applied to the bronze largely obtained by the Romans from that island, but also mined elsewhere.

The term Cyprian, in addition denoting an inhabitant or native of Cyprus was, in the 19th century, a synonym for a dissolute, licentious person.

Corinth of Corinthian. The once great Greek city of Corinth, on the

Gulf of Corinth, west of Athens, was notorious for its luxury and sensuousness, so that in former times the term Corinthian was applied to a man of pleasure and fashion.

The name survives to-day in the famous amateur Association football team, the Corinthians, who have produced some of the greatest players in the history of the sport.

Corinthian architecture, distinguished by bell-shaped capitals with rows of leaves of the acanthus (the Bear's Breech or architect's plant), was one of the three Greek and five classical orders of architecture. The others were Doric, Ionic, Tuscan and Composite.

Covent Garden of Covent Garden. Covent Garden, which name is a corruption of Convent Garden, lies between the Strand and Oxford Street, London, and was originally the site of the garden of the Abbot of Westminster. The square was laid out and the adjacent church of St. Paul designed, by Inigo Jones (*c.* 1573–1652). It became a fashionable residential quarter and is frequently mentioned in literature.

To-day the name immediately implies to the general public the great fruit, vegetable and flower market which occupies the site, the greatest market of its kind in the British Isles and probably in the world.

The adjacent Opera House, or the Covent Garden Theatre and Royal Opera House, is the focus of British grand opera. The original Opera House was built in 1732. Increased prices levied to pay for the costs of a later rebuilding, after the fire of 1808, led to the Old Price Riots. For some years during last century it was known as the Royal Italian Opera House. It has not been used entirely for Grand Opera, to which international celebrities have contributed, but has a notable record of stage performance. Many great actors and actresses and managers, including Garrick, Peg

Woffington, Kemble and Macready appeared there.

The present building, erected in 1858, is almost semicircular and holds 2,000 people.

In recent years arrangements between the governing syndicate and the British Broadcasting Corporation have done much to ensure continuity of success and sustained economic production.

Coventry of Coventry true blue, "To send to Coventry." Coventry, the cathedral city in Warwickshire, which was made a separate diocese in 1918, is popularly familiar through the 11th-century Lady Godiva story. There is a prominent post-Second War Statue of her by Sir William Reid Dick.

Coventry is a great industrial centre, formerly celebrated for its broad-cloth, woollens, etc. Its Mystery Miracle Plays are of very ancient origin and were played before royalty in the 15th century. Also Coventry was the seat of Parliament.

The expression "Coventry true blue" referred to a particular local thread of the 17th century. The city, which was severely bombed in the Second World War, is now primarily concerned with machinery, electrical goods, cars, iron foundries, bicycles, weaving, materials, etc.

The expression "To send to Coventry," meaning to banish a person from the society or circle of which he or she is a member, as a mark of disapproval or disgust, is attributed to several sources.

Some accounts say that it arose because at one time citizens so disliked the military that any woman seen speaking to a soldier was boycotted. Others suggest that troublesome soldiers or suspect prisoners in the Civil wars were sent to the Parliamentary stronghold of the Coventry garrison party. Other records associate the phrase with an originating reference in Clarendon's *Historical*

Narrative of the Rebellion and Civil Wars in England (1702–4).

The expression is used with a similar meaning in the United States and was so employed by Emerson (1803–82) in his *Essays*.

Croatia of Cravat. Croatia-Slavonia, formerly a crownland in the Austro-Hungarian Empire, and now a province of Jugoslavia, is responsible for the word cravat, meaning a type of neckcloth or tie, particularly fashionable in the 17th–19th centuries.

It is said to have owed its popularity to its introduction into France by Croatian soldiers in the 17th century. A French regiment modelled on Croat lines embodied the unusual neckcloths in its uniform.

The fashion was popular in Britain and the tie is mentioned in Butler's *Hudibras* (1663–78).

Cremona of Cremona violins. The capital city and province of Cremona is in Lombardy, Northern Italy. It is a cathedral city and supports a considerable industry in textiles, produce and wines. In earlier centuries it was noted for a distinguished school of painters and even more celebrated for its violins which were, and are, unsurpassed.

Andrea and Nicolo Amati (the brothers) were the originators of the Cremona school in the 16th century. The great family of violin makers named Guarneri lived at Cremona, which was also the workplace of the great pupil of Nicolo Amati, Antonio Stradivari (1644–1737).

Creton of Cretonne. The fabric cretonne, a stout, unglazed cotton cloth with a pattern printed on one or both sides, perhaps but not certainly derives its name from the Normandy village of Creton. It was originally manufactured there and in other places and its first form was a strong, white fabric with a linen weft and hemp woof. It was introduced about 1865 as a competitor to the thinner chintz for curtains, furniture coverings, etc.

Curaçao of Curaçao. The famous liqueur, curaçao (or curaçoa), derives from the Dutch West Indies island of Curaçao, which lies off the north coast of Venezuela, South America.

It produces sugar, tobacco, chemicals, cattle, etc. The liqueur, which is manufactured in the island and more extensively in Holland, depends largely for its characteristics upon the essence and distillation of the peel of the Curaçao orange.

The Curassow, or Cracinæ, which also derives its name from the island, is a turkey-like, handsome game bird common to the tropical forests of South America. It can be domesticated. Some species are curiously crested.

Dalmatia of Dalmatian and Dalmatic. The Yugoslavian province of Dalmatia, on the western Adriatic seaboard, was the original breeding place of the Dalmatian dogs which are characterized by round black or liver spots and are popularly known as the "Plum pudding dogs."

The breed was used in Dalmatia and surrounding countries primarily as a gun dog but its popular introduction into this country last century was in the capacity of carriage dog. It would run under the rear axle of a carriage and was in fact alternatively known as the Coach or Carriage dog. The breed appears in a number of paintings of the period.

Dalmatia also gave its name to the ecclesiastical vestment known as the dalmatic. It is worn by deacons assisting at Mass, by certain other officials on particular occasions and by bishops. It has a similar straight front and back, is placed over the head and the sleeves are little more than shoulders, leaving the arms free. It is generally marked with two stripes from the shoulder to the base of the vestment on front and back. It is worn over the alb and corresponds to the chasuble of the Celebrant.

The garment, which appears to have evolved from a Dalmatian royal vest, is still used at Coronation ceremonies, here and in other countries.

Damascus of Damask, Damascus road, etc. Damascus, the capital of Syria (*Isa. vii. 8*), is mentioned frequently in the Bible and was one of the oldest oriental cities. The vast plain of Damascus is extremely fertile. The city includes the Gate of God, through which the pilgrimage to Mecca (*q.v.*) sets out. The "street called Straight" (*Acts ix. 11*) runs through Damascus and it was on the Damascus road that Paul's conversion took place (*Acts ix. 1–25*). Therefrom the phrase "a Damascus road" is applied to a spiritual climacteric in a person's life.

Damask was the term originally applied to rich figured silks manufactured in Damascus, but it now includes woollen and other fabrics with woven patterns seen by light reflection. The industry was originally carried to Byzantium by the Crusaders, whence it passed to Italy and France. It was brought to England by the Flemish weavers who escaped from the persecution of the Duke of Alva in the 16th century. Damasks are now manufactured in many parts of the British Isles.

Damascus steel, first manufactured in the city, was notable for a wavy or watered surface pattern secured by a welding of iron and steel. Many of the Damascus blades were richly ornamented and often inlaid with precious metals, which gave rise to the term damascene, or damasceening.

The small dark purple plum known as the damson is named from the city.

Dan of Dan to Beersheba. The expression "From Dan to Beersheba," signifying extreme limits, as does "From Land's End to John o' Groats" (*q.v.*) in relation to the British Isles, is of Biblical origin (*Judges xx. 1*, etc.). It implied the span from one end of the kingdom to the other, or all over the world. The places represented the most northern and most southern cities of the Promised Land. The Tribe of Dan was the last tribe to receive its portion of the Kingdom (*Josh. xix. 40–8*).

Professor George Saintsbury describes Butler's *Anatomy of Melancholy* (1621) as "a wandering of the soul from Dan to Beersheba."

Darien of the Darien Scheme. The

Isthmus of Darien is better known to-day as Panama, severed by the vital, arterial Panama Canal.

The Darien Scheme was the project of William Paterson, founder of the Bank of England, who in 1695 projected a settlement on the Isthmus domination. Scottish compatriots of the originator sailed to found the New St. Andrews.

The Spaniards offered opposition and defeated the colonists, who were ill equipped to stand the onslaught and the ravages of the climate.

Work was begun on the Panama Canal, which had been advocated for several centuries, in 1881.

The name Darien is well known in literature through Keats' famous lines:

Or like stout Cortez, when with eagle eyes
He stared at the Pacific—and all his men
Look'd at each other with a wild surmise—
Silent upon a peak in Darien.

On first looking into
Chapman's Homer.

Dartmoor of Dartmoor. The south-west plateau of Dartmoor, Devonshire, is used in addition to its topographical significance, as referring to the great convict prison at Princetown, in an isolated part of the moor. It was built for French prisoners in 1809 and was put to its present use in 1855.

Delphi of the Delphic Oracle. Delphi, or Delphos, was a town on the slopes of Mount Parnassus, in ancient Greece. It was the site of a temple to Apollo and contained the Delphic oracle, the most famous of all oracles. Its pronouncements brought vast riches to the temple and were of such wide influence as to cause the continued application of the phrase to any spectacular source of prophecy or to the prophet.

The Delphic Oracle was primarily concerned with religious questions, the human placation of the gods and the averting of evil.

Delphi was regarded as "the navel of the world" and the pronouncements of the oracle were of supreme power during the 8th to the 5th centuries B.C. Its waning influence continued until the 4th century A.D.

Shakespeare cites Delphos as an island in *The Winter's Tale*:

I have dispatch'd in post
To sacred Delphos, to Apollo's temple,
Cleomenes and Dion . . . (ii. 1).

Cleomenes and Dion . . . are both landed.
(ii. 3).

Nîmes of Denim. The cotton twill fabric known as denim was originally known as *serge de Nîmes*, from the capital city of the French department of Gard, in the south, near Marseilles. It is a cathedral city with notable Roman ruins. It was the home of the distinguished French novelist, Alphonse Daudet (1840–97). Nîmes has a large trade in wines, spirits, textiles and machinery.

The word denims was widely used during and after the Second World War when the material, in dungaree form, was a service issue officially called denims and used for manual training and exercises.

Dungaree, which is a coarse Indian calico, derives its name from the Hindu equivalent *dungri*. It is also, from its use therein, the legged, overall working garment.

Demerara of Demerara sugar. The brown, granulated sugar known as Demerara comes from the county of that name in British Guiana, South America. Georgetown stands at the mouth of the river of the same name.

The principal exports are sugar and molasses and there is a considerable trade in gold, diamonds, coffee, etc.

Derbyshire of Derbyshire neck or goitre. The midland county of Derbyshire is notable for mining, potteries, iron and steel, etc., and scenically for the famous Peak districts. Its county town is the seat of a bishop. Haddon Hall and Chatsworth House, the latter the seat of the Duke of

Devonshire, are two of the most famous mansions in Britain.

Goitre, the affection of the thyroid gland which causes considerable swelling of the front of the neck, was known as Derbyshire neck because of its prevalence in the county. It was at one time thought to be due to deficiencies in the water of the area. The disease, which is less prevalent to-day and more susceptible to increased medical knowledge, is found in many countries.

Shakespeare is believed to refer to the unsightly condition occasioned by goitre in *The Tempest, iii. 3.*

Who would believe that there were mountaineers
Dew-lapp'd like bulls, whose throats had hanging at them
Wallets of flesh?

Digby of Digby chick. The county and town of Digby, in Nova Scotia, on the Canadian Atlantic seaboard, is occupied with coal and minerals but is particularly noted for its herring fishery. The name Digby, or Digby chick, for the smoked herring, is widely known.

Damietta of Dimity. The Egyptian town of Damietta, lies between the right bank of the Nile and Lake Menzaleh. It is claimed by some authorities to be the origin of the word dimity. Others aver that the cotton fabric with raised stripes derives its name from *di-mitos*, double or warped thread. Dimity is used in some parts of Cornwall to describe the twilight.

The rich, mediæval dress material, samite, in which the weft-threads are caught at every sixth warp-thread, has a comparable origin from *hexamitum*.

Samite is known chiefly to the general public through Tennyson's line in *Idylls of the King* (1859): "Clothed in white samite, mystic, wonderful." The line appears also in *Morte d'Arthur* which was the genesis of the *Idylls.*

Dicte of Dittany On the slopes of the mountain of Dicte, or Dikte, in Crete, the herb dittany flourished and was named therefrom. It is mentioned by Milton and other poets and was used extensively in herbal medicine, particularly for cleansing and stanching wounds.

Doctors' Commons of Doctors' Commons. Though the society of Doctors' Commons no longer exists and its building has been destroyed, references to it are so frequent in literature and history that it should be explained. The name was given to a society of ecclesiastical lawyers, a distinct branch of the legal professions concerned with civil and canon laws. The Commons arose from the community boarding facilities offered and required of members in the college. It was situated on the south side of St. Paul's Churchyard, London, near the College of Arms. It was destroyed in the Great Fire, 1666, but rebuilt. The church, through the Archbishop of Canterbury, had much administrative power over Doctors' Commons and the president was the Dean of the Arches. The Court of the Arches still sits on ecclesiastical matters.

The college was dissolved and the property sold in 1867, but traces of the association are still found in local names.

Marriage licences were granted by the college and at one time the district acquired some of the disrepute associated with the notorious Fleet marriages (*q.v.*).

Donnybrook Fair of Donnybrook Fair. From the time of King John, who established annual fairs there, until the middle of last century, Donnybrook, an ancient village near Dublin, Eire, was each year the scene of riotous hilarity and notorious disorder. As a result the name became synonymous with an occasion of disorder and general rioting.

The village now forms a suburb of Dublin.

Doris of Dorian, Doric. Doris, a pastoral area of ancient Greece, gave rise to Dorian and Doric applied to the inhabitants of the region, to their rustic dialect and to one of the three classic Grecian orders of architecture. The Doric column is a severely plain fluted pillar. A simple yet dignified form of early Church music is known as the Dorian Mode.

Douai of the Douai Bible. The French town of Douai, in the Department du Nord, is associated with the translation from the Vulgate which was made by English Roman Catholic scholars in France during the 17th century for the use of English ordinands.

The New Testament was published at Rheims in 1582 and the Old Testament at Douai in 1609. It is sometimes called the Rheims-Douai version and among the specially named editions it is cited as the Rosin Bible because of the translation of *Jer. viii. 22* as "Is there no rosin in Galaad." The Authorized Version (1611) translates the word as "balm."

The Geneva Bible, which included many important revisions and typographical improvements, was published from the Swiss city in 1560. Its special name is the Breeches Bible, because the passage in *Gen. iii. 7* reads "they sowed fig-tree leaves together and made themselves breeches."

Dowlas of Dowlas. A coarse, unbleached linen or calico of great endurance was known as Dowlas from the Brittany village of that name. It is seen less frequently nowadays but at one time was used extensively for working garments and aprons on account of its durability. Linen drapers were frequently called "Mr. Dowlas."

Shakespeare mentions the word in *1 Henry IV, iii. 3*, when Falstaff refers to a dozen shirts bought by Mistress Quickly as: "Dowlas, filthy dowlas: I have given them away to bakers' wives, and they have made bolters of them."

A bolter was a sieve or sifter.

Downing Street of Downing Street. The term "Downing Street" is popularly synonymous with pronouncements by the Prime Minister or policy or statements of Cabinet authority.

No. 10 Downing Street is the Prime Minister's official London residence and as such the scene of many historic meetings and decisions.

The street, which leads off Whitehall, near the Cenotaph, is named from Sir George Downing, a soldier and diplomat of the reign of Charles II. He was member for Morpeth for many years.

No. 11 Downing Street is the residence of the Chancellor of the Exchequer, and No. 12 the office of Government Whips.

The country residence of the Prime Minister, Chequers, is a Tudor house in the Chilterns, near Princes Risborough, Bucks. It was an endowed gift to the nation for that purpose in 1921 from Lord and Lady Lee of Fareham. Chequers is surrounded by a large estate and includes a notable art collection.

Dresden of Dresden China. The German city of Dresden, capital of Saxony, lies in the valley of the Elbe. It is an extensive railway centre. It has a world famous art collection and many great musicians have been associated with the city.

Dresden's manufacture of china and ornaments in fine metal has been famous there for several centuries. At certain periods Dresden repairers of porcelain were also counterfeiters of notable pieces that came into their hands.

Drogheda of Drugget. Drogheda, the Irish seaport on the banks of the Boyne, is given by some authorities as the origin of drugget, the coarse floorcovering. Drogheda had a flourishing textile industry in earlier days, part of which has been revived. Linen and damask are made there.

Other claims are also made that the name derives from the French *droguet*, applied to the same material.

Drury Lane of Drury Lane. The term Drury Lane is still used to imply the peak of theatrical enterprise and production. The lane, which is between Covent Garden and the Strand, London, was named after a Tudor family of Drury which owned a large house there. The Theatre Royal, popularly known as "Drury Lane," has been rebuilt several times since the original cockpit days. Wren was the architect in the 1674 rebuilding. Many of the greatest actors and actresses have appeared there and it has been the scene of some of the most spectacular productions and outstanding successes. It is a notable theatre for pantomime.

Duffel of Duffel. The coarse woollen cloth with a heavy nap, known as Duffel, takes the name from its original manufacture at the Belgian town of Duffel in the Brabant, southeast of Antwerp. The name, in the expression "duffel coats," was used extensively during and after the Second World War when heavy coats of this and similar materials were a Service issue subsequently favoured by civilians.

Tennyson uses the phrase "good duffel gray."

Dam-Dama of Dum-Dum. The town of Dam-Dama, or Dum-Dum, near Fort William, in the Province of Bengal, India, was the headquarters of the Bengal artillery and noted for its cantonment and arsenal. Here were first manufactured the dum-dum bullets which came into prominence during the Boer War.

Their characteristic was a soft nose which expanded on contact, causing a lacerated wound and thus increasing the bullets' destructive powers.

The town was prominent in the Indian Mutiny in 1857.

Dunmow of the Dunmow Flitch. Great Dunmow, the market town in Essex, noted for the Dunmow Flitch, is situated on the Chelmer, ten miles west of Braintree. It has a population of 3,000. Little Dunmow, a tiny village 2 miles distant, where the ceremony was originally held, possesses the remains of an Augustinian Priory. The Prior's Chair, once used in the Flitch ceremony, is in the parish church which is part of the original priory.

It is claimed that the Dunmow Flitch of Bacon was instituted in 1244 by Robert de Fitzwalter, who revived the Dunmow Priory. It was to be the prize for any married couple who could go to the priory, and kneeling on two sharp pointed stones, swear that they had not quarrelled nor repented of their marriage within a year and a day after its celebration.

There is a record of the award in 1445, to Richard Wright, a labourer from Badbury, Norfolk, but the custom was clearly established long before that time as it is mentioned in Langland's *The Vision of Piers the Plowman* which is dated about 1362. The Flitch is also mentioned in Chaucer's *Canterbury Tales* (about 1387), in the Prologue of the *Wife of Bath's Tale*.

In 1778, a ballad opera, *The Flitch of Bacon*, was produced at the Haymarket. Its author was Henry Bate (afterwards Sir Henry Bate Dudley), the son of a clergyman in the Chelmsford district.

Harrison Ainsworth (1805–82) did much to revive the popularity of the custom. His novel, *The Flitch of Bacon* (1842), caused a local committee to meet to revive the custom which had been followed sporadically through the centuries. The novelist offered to present a Flitch for the next summer and to contribute five guineas towards the expenses of the festivities which had always marked the public trial and award.

Applications were invited for this presentation Flitch in July, 1855, and two couples were selected, Mr. and Mrs. James Barlow, of Chipping Ongar, and Chevalier and Mme de Chatelain. The latter pair were distinguished in contemporary literature.

Both couples were adjudged to have justified their claim, and the Harrison Flitch was presented by the donor to the Chevalier and Mme de Chatelain in Windmill Field, "with due solemnity."

Ainsworth wrote a long poem entitled *The Custom of Dunmow* and there are descriptive verses by Mme de Chatelain and other poets.

There are records of a similar custom, which persists at Dunmow, at Whichnor, Staffs, and in Germany and France.

E

Eccles of Eccles Cakes. Eccles, the Lancashire borough and suburb of Manchester, with which city it was incorporated in 1892, supports a considerable engineering and textile industry but is known more widely for the flat, spiced Eccles cakes which are made extensively in the district and, on similar lines, elsewhere.

Eden of the Garden of Eden. The use of the expression "Eden" or "The Garden of Eden" to imply a place of bliss or a state of supreme happiness, derives from the *Genesis* story of the Creation. The reference is *Gen. ii. 8–17*: "And the Lord God planted a garden eastward in Eden . . ." and put the man "into the garden of Eden to dress it and keep it."

Edinburgh of Edinburgh Rock. Edinburgh, the capital of Scotland, is dominated by the ancient castle and Holyrood Palace. It is a University city, famous for its historical, literary, artistic and scientific associations and present activities. *The Edinburgh Review*, founded in 1802 and first edited by Sydney Smith, is notable for literary annals, particularly for fierce criticisms of Wordsworth and Southey. It ceased publication in 1929.

Edinburgh Rock, the famous sweet, was first manufactured in the city by Alexander Ferguson, Ltd., in 1822, and was so named from the towering castle rock which was within a stone's throw of the originator's premises at 72 West Bow.

The chief industry of this cultural rather than commercial city to-day is ale brewing. There is also a considerable amount of publishing and book-making.

"Auld Reekie," the name applied to Edinburgh old town, was given because the district was smoke-ridden and generally appeared to be clouded by a reek of smoke.

The Edinburgh Festival, inaugurated after the Second World War, has become a musical and dramatic event of world importance.

El Dorado of El Dorado. The term El Dorado, to imply the unattainable but ever-sought goal of human happiness, is a fiction that was for many years regarded as an actual place. The name, from the Spanish, *The Golden*, was applied to a gleaming city long believed to exist in the South American interior. It was said to be the city of Manoa and mapped on the descriptions of Martinez until its existence was disproved by Humboldt (1769–1859), the German naturalist and explorer.

El Dorado was believed by Raleigh and others to be a city on the banks of the Amazon or the Orinoco.

The name appears frequently in literature and was chosen by several cities in the United States, notably in the pioneer days of the oil-fields.

Elysium of Elysian. Elysium was a place in the mental and spiritual sense in Greek mythology. It is the origin of the frequently used adjective Elysian. It was the Islands of the Blest, where those whom the gods favoured enjoyed a life of serenity. In earliest accounts it appears to have been a place separate from Hades. It was ruled over by Rhadamanthus, son of Zeus and Europa.

The Elysian fields was the paradise of Greek mythology.

For Elysians the sun seems always to have just set.
Disraeli, *The Infernal Marriage* (1834).

> *This life of mortal breath*
> *Is but a suburb of the life Elysian,*
> *Whose portal we call Death.*
> Longfellow, *Resignation.*

47

Nirvana, a term favoured by poets and ballad-makers, is the Buddhist beatitude; a blowing out or extinction of individuality with absorption into the supreme, all-pervading spirit.

Ettrick of "The Ettrick Shepherd." James Hogg (1770–1835), the Border poet who was known as "The Ettrick Shepherd," was born in Ettrick which stands on the river of the same name in Selkirkshire, Scotland. Hogg was for many years a shepherd whose poetical gifts were discovered by Scott. The shepherd supplied the novelist with much material for his *Border Minstrelsy* (1802–3).

Hogg, who wrote notable verse and ballads, enjoyed the company of Byron, Wordsworth and other leading writers of the time. He contributed to the *Noctes Ambrosianæ* and was the "Ettrick Shepherd" in these imaginary conversations which appeared in *Blackwood's Magazine*, 1822–35.

F

Faenza of Faience. The ancient cathedral town of Faenza is situated in northern Italy, south-east of Bologna.

Here was first made the earthenware and porcelain subsequently known as faience. Majolica ware (*q.v.*) is also manufactured there, and there are silk and allied textile industries.

Fair Isle of Fair Isle Knitting. The small island of Fair Isle is in the Shetland group, south-west of Sumburgh head, which is the southern extremity of the Shetland mainland. It has an area of only three square miles and is mainly rocky. The industries of its few hundred inhabitants are fishing and knitting. The intricate and many coloured patterns of their products are famous and are believed to derive from Moorish traditions and designs brought to the island by the crew of a vessel of the Spanish Armada wrecked off the island in 1588.

The name is now applied to many garments and patterns of similar type made elsewhere.

Falernus of Falerian Wine. Horace (65–8 B.C.) described Falerian as surpassing all wines and it was highly esteemed by the connoisseurs of ancient Rome. It was made, both sweet and dry, from grapes grown at Falernus, a district north of Naples in the district of Campagna.

Fastnet Rock of the Fastnet Race. The famous handicapped race for small yachts, from Cowes to the Fastnet and back to Plymouth, a distance of some 600 miles, takes its name from the Fastnet Rock. It is marked by a lighthouse and stands four miles south-west of Cape Clear, off Clear Island, south-west of Baltimore, Co. Cork, Eire.

St. Fiacre Hotel of the Fiacre. The French cab known as the fiacre was named from the Hotel de St. Fiacre, in Paris, where the vehicles first appeared in the 17th century. It figures frequently in contemporary literature and art.

St. Fiacre, whose day is August 30, is thought to have been the son of a 7th-century king of Ireland. He became an anchorite, founding a monastery at Breuil, in France. In the 16th century his remains were removed to the Cathedral of Meaux, in northern France. Miracles were attributed to him and to his shrine.

Fingal's Cave of *Fingal's Cave Overture*. The tiny island of Staffa, Argyllshire, near Iona and Mull, is volcanic in origin and noted for its caves.

One of the most famous is Fingal's Cave, reputed to have been the dwelling place of Fingal, the ancient, possibly mythological, Gaelic hero who was father of Ossian. The poems attributed to Ossian, including an epic entitled *Fingal*, were presented as authentic by James Macpherson (1736–96). Their authenticity was the subject of a famous controversy between the sponsor and Dr. Johnson.

Mendelssohn (1809–47) visited the Hebrides, including Staffa, in 1829. In Fingal's Cave he is said to have thought of the chief theme of *Fingal's Cave Overture*, or *The Hebrides*. It was three years before it was performed.

Fleet Prison of Fleet Marriages. Fleet Prison, on the east side of Farringdon Street, London, E.C. occupied the site of Fleet Market. The

Fleet River ran near by, joining the Holbourne and entering the Thames at Blackfriars Bridge, as it can still be seen to do, though as a sewer.

The ancient prison had been rebuilt many times and was destroyed in the Fire of London, 1666. It was destroyed just over a century later in the Gordon Riots.

The keeper of the prison, which housed many distinguished prisoners, including Penn and Wycherley, was called the Warden of the Fleet.

The unlicensed marriage practice, which seems to have started with one or two London incumbents who claimed to be outside the jurisdiction of the Bishop of London, was taken up profitably by clerical prisoners in the Fleet. Many are named in old records, including one known as "The Bishop of Hell." It is said that some of the ministers made as much as £500 a year by this practice.

The marriages were first celebrated in the chapel of the prison, but when legislation prohibited marriages in chapels without banns, the prison precincts were profitably employed, as were adjacent taverns.

Fleet Marriages were declared by law to be void in 1753. The bill met much opposition and was, according to Horace Walpole, "crammed down the throats of both Houses, though they gave many a gulp before they could swallow it." (See *Gretna Green*.)

Fleet Street of Fleet Street. The term Fleet Street, used to symbolize journalism, derives from the newspaper and allied offices concentrated in the short thoroughfare. It runs from the Griffon (which replaced Temple Bar) at the east end of the Strand to Ludgate Circus. It has been called "The Street of Adventure" and "The Street of Ink," and though many newspaper organizations are now not actually in Fleet Street it remains the focus of the profession and many of the great national daily papers and most of the leading

provincial newspapers have offices there.

St. Bride's Church, the Wren building with the famous "wedding-cake" spire, was known as Fleet Street's cathedral. Henley described the spire as a madrigal in stone. The church was almost completely destroyed by bombing during the Second World War, but the damaged spire survives. The other church, St. Dunstan's in the West, is notable for its octagonal shape and for the memorials to many figures in literature. Of the previous church on the site John Donne (1572–1631) was rector, Izaak Walton an earnest parishioner.

Fleet Street contains many famous taverns and coffee houses, notably the Cheshire Cheese, which Dr. Johnson frequented, and the Cock. At one time Fleet Street extended westwards to the Savoy (*q.v.*).

Florence of Florin. Florence, the city and province of Central Italy, is where the first florin was struck, in the 11th century. The coin, a gold piece, was called a "florence" and the appositeness of the name was accentuated by the flower, a lily, in the obverse design.

The florin was much used in European trade and many countries, including England, incorporated it in their coinage. It has been of gold and silver and of varying values.

Queen Victoria issued a silver florin in 1849—value two shillings. It was known as the Graceless Florin because the words *Dei Gratia* were omitted from the inscription. The words were inserted three years later. A double florin, issued in 1887, was withdrawn in 1890.

The florin of to-day, of debased silver, is still legal tender for two shillings.

Frascati of Frascati. The hills surrounding Rome are covered with vineyards and olive groves and it is here that many famous wines are produced, including Frascati, noted since the days of Horace (65–8 B.C.), who praised frequently the wine of Tusculum (Frascati).

Frascati, a popular resort noted for many famous villas, is 1,000 ft. above sea level and south-east of Rome. The wine is a mellow golden yellow and is made in two types, dry and demi-sweet or fruity. Other noted wines of the Latium province are Velletri, Marino and Est-Est-Est Montefiascone. The latter is produced in the neighbourhood of Lake Bolsena.

A delightful tradition, still told, concerning the latter wine, goes back to the 11th century. Then Emperor Henry V visited Rome and among his retinue was one John Defuk. Defuk attached so much importance to good wines, and his enjoyment of them, that he sent a servant ahead of the main party to test the vintage possibilities of each district. He was required by Defuk to record the word "Est" on the door of each inn where he found the wine was good and likely to satisfy his master.

When the servant came to Montefiascone he found such superb wine that he marked the door of the inn: "Est! Est! Est!"

Defuk fully endorsed the tribute, stayed several days to enjoy the wine, and after the Rome pilgrimage returned to Montefiascone to spend the rest of his life there.

By the connoisseur's will the Municipality was left his carriage and horses and a sum of money to provide that each year, on the anniversary of Defuk's death, a barrel of the glorious local wine should be poured upon his grave.

Defuk was buried in the cathedral of S. Flaviano Martyr and his tomb bears the inscription *Est Est Est Propter Nimium Est Huc Jo. Defuk Dominus Meus Mortuus est.*

France of French Leave, etc. To take French leave, *i.e.* leave without authority or notice, is one of many instances of a euphemistic courtesy associated particularly with the French. In this case it was coined by the English, following a habit intimately associated with France. An instance is their naming a prostitute a *fille de joie*. Venereal disease was at one time commonly called "French gout." A counter-action in France was to call a creditor *Un Anglais*.

The term "poodle-faking," to denote an absurd, superficial deception —"mutton dressed as lamb," for example—is a shortened form of "French poodle-faking." These dogs, with their clipped, sometimes pomaded, unnatural appearance, are symptomatic of an extreme exploitation of dog-fancying which reaches its height in certain districts of Paris. There it is possible to purchase dogs equipped with jackets with handkerchief in pocket and even provided with diapers for the pre-house-trained period. Even chastity belts are procurable—a dog's life.

The name French is also found in French horn (an instrument in the trumpet family), French chalk, polish, drain (a rubble soakaway), windows (folding glass outer doors), etc.

Frisian Islands of Friesian cattle. The Frisian islands extend along the north coast of Holland and the Dutch province of Friesland, or Vriesland is adjacent on the north-east coast of the Zuider Zee. The Frisians are noted for cattle rearing and allied industries. There is also an extensive textile manufacture.

Fustat of Fustian. Fustat, or Fostat, the suburb of Cairo, gives its name to a word which has to-day largely surrendered its primary meaning. It was, and still is, a thick twilled, short napped cotton cloth, of the velveteen, corduroy class. It is usually dyed a dark colour.

In the Middle Ages it was used for comely apparel and for church vestments. To-day it is associated with artisan wear.

The more frequent use of the word fustian to-day is to imply something shoddy and pretentious. It can be applied to speech or manner.

Discourse fustian with one's own shadow.
Othello, ii. 3.

And he whose fustian's so sublimely bad,
It is not poetry, but prose run mad.
Pope, *Prologue to the Satires.*

G

Galilee of Galilee porch. At the time of Christ Galilee embraced most of northern Palestine. The term Galilee porch is applied architecturally to porches or chapels attached to churches or cathedrals. They were frequently reserved for meetings in which the main building could not be used, such as the gathering of monks with women relatives who were precluded from the abbey, as lych chapels for coffins awaiting the funeral ceremonies, and for penitents, etc.

Galilee, which means a ring or circuit, in this case referring to the mountains surrounding the plain, was called "the Galilee of the Gentiles" (*Matt. iv. 15*). The term was perhaps applied to the porch as being less sacred than the main building by comparison with Galilee as opposed to Judea, the southern part of Palestine which included Bethlehem, the birthplace of Christ (*Matt. ii. 1–5*) and was the scene of the ministrations of John the Baptist (*Matt. iii. 1*).

Cambodia of Gamboge. The province of Cambodia is in French Indo China, flanked on the west by Siam. Here was first obtained the yellow pigment from the resin of trees originally grown in Cambodia and now also extensively grown in Siam, Ceylon, etc.

Gamboge is used in certain medical preparations as a purgative.

Gath of "Tell it not in Gath . . ." Gath, which name means a wine vat, was a city of Philistines, on the borders of Judah and Philistia. It was the reputed birthplace of Goliath, the Philistine giant who defied the armies of Israel for forty days until he was slain by David (*1 Sam. xvii. 4*).

The expression, still frequently used to imply that information should not be given to enemies nor disseminated unwisely, derives from David's lament over Saul and Jonathan, his son, *2 Sam. i. 20*: "Tell it not in Gath, publish it not in the streets of Askelon; lest the daughters of the Philistines rejoice, lest the daughters of the uncircumcized triumph."

The famous passage includes the oft used phrase: "How are the mighty fallen, and the weapons of war perished."

Askelon, one of the five cities of the Philistines, was on the Mediterranean, just north of Gaza.

It has another echo in our language for it was famous for a kind of onion called *ascaloniæ* in mediæval times. It was favoured in France, where it was called *échalotes*. The onion, still popular, is our shalot, or shallot.

Gap of Gavotte. Gap, the French town near the Cottian Alps on the Italian frontier, is thought to be the origin of the word gavotte. It comes from Gavots, the local name of the inhabitants of the district, where the form perhaps originated.

The gavotte is a lively dance, not unlike the minuet, with two repeated sections. The form has been utilized by many distinguished composers.

Gaza of Gauze. Gaza, now called Ghuzzeh, the Palestinian city on the Mediterranean shore, is generally accepted as the origin of the word gauze, the light transparent material which was first made there.

Gaza was the most southerly of the five chief cities of ancient Palestine. It is mentioned frequently in the Bible, also under the name of Azzah, and is largely familiar to the public owing to association with Samson. He carried away the gates of the town (*Judges xvi. 1–3*) and was imprisoned there. It was at Gaza that he was blinded and pulled down the temple of Dagon upon himself and upon the Philistines, more than 3,000 of whom were slain (*Judges xvi. 4–31*).

Gaza was one of the five Philistine cities that gave golden trespass-offering to the Lord (*1 Sam. vi. 17*).

Aldous Huxley used the title *Eyeless in Gaza* for a novel in 1935.

Hinnom of Gehenna. Used as a synonym for hell, or a place of torment and everlasting destruction, the name Gehenna derives from the Hebrew *gehinnom*, from the valley of Hinnom. The ravine south of Jerusalem was where the Jews sacrificed to Molech, or Moloch, and Baal. "Ahaz . . . made molten images for Baalim . . . and burnt his children in the fire, after the abomination of the heathen" (*2 Chron. xxviii. 1–3*).

After the Exile the valley became the sewer of the city.

The word "Hell" appears frequently in the New Testament as the symbol of eternal damnation

Milton (1608–74) refers to Hinnom as Gehenna, the type of hell, in *Paradise Lost, Book One.*

Geneva of Geneva Cross, Geneva Gown. The canton and city of Geneva in Switzerland contains a cathedral and notable museums. The academy founded by Calvin (1509–64), the reformer who made Geneva the religious centre of Europe, is now the University. Geneva was chosen as the site of the League of Nations Headquarters in 1927. Its main industries are watch and clock manufacture, jewellery and diamond cutting.

The Red Cross organization, which evolved from the Geneva conventions of 1864 and 1906, adopted as its now world-wide symbol, the insignia of the ancient Order of St. John which had long been noted for its life-saving activities. The Red Greek Cross on a white ground became known as the Geneva Cross.

The gowns and bands, worn by Calvinists, and still worn by some evangelical clergy, are known by the adjective Geneva.

Gin, the spirit, is more correctly called Geneva, but is not to be confused with the Swiss city. It is a corruption from the Old French *genevre*, or juniper, the shrub yielding the oil with which the malt distillation is flavoured to make gin. The spirit is made in many countries, including Holland, hence the term Hollands in connection with gin.

Schiedam, or schnapps, is manufactured at Schiedam, the centre of the Hollands Dutch gin industry, a few miles west of Rotterdam. Schnapps is generally made from rye and malt, with the characteristic juniper flavouring.

Genoa of Genoa cake. The rich, almond-topped cake known as Genoa takes its name from the city and province in north-west of Italy. For centuries famed for its arts, Genoa is now also a great commercial city and port of international strategic importance.

Christopher Columbus was born at or near Genoa about 1436. Sir William Watson (1858–1935) called him the "indomitable soul, immortal Genoese."

Gethsemane of the Garden of Gethsemane. The olive garden at the foot of the Mount of Olives was often visited by Christ and it was the scene of His Agony and Betrayal (*Mark xiv. 32–46*). The name means an oil press.

The phrase has come to be applied to a person's ordeal of anguish of mind and body.

Gilead of "Is there no balm in Gilead?" The expression "Is there no balm in Gilead? Is there no physician there?" (*Jer. viii. 22*) is still widely used to imply that there must be some remedy or consolation for present desolation. The phrase is also used in a positive sense: "balm in

Gilead" denoting any welcome palliative for, or solution to, an arid situation.

Gilead, the hill of testimony, and the Land of Gilead, were on the east of Jordan. The fertile, mountainous country was noted for a precious balm, or balsam, a resinous product of local trees with a celebrated reputation for its medicinal properties. The balm formed a valuable and extensive product in the merchandise of the Arab and Phoenician merchants.

Shakespeare, using the word balm in several of the historical plays, applies it to the oil of consecration.

Goa of Goa Powder. Araroba, the astringent powder known as Goa, is used in medicine, particularly for the treatment of certain skin diseases. It is named from its place of origin, Goa, the Portuguese settlement on the west coast of India. In earlier days this town on the Malabar coast was a notable trading centre.

The yellow powder is found in holes in the trunks of a tree of South American origin.

The Cedar of Goa is unconnected with the Town and is believed to have been introduced to Britain from Mexico, via Portugal; possibly with the aid of Goa merchants.

Golconda of Golconda. The use of the term Golconda, to typify a mine of wealth or endless treasure, derives from the ancient city so named near Hyderabad. Golconda was the former name of the present state of southern India.

The city was once capital of a powerful and wealthy kingdom and the centre of an extensive diamond cutting and polishing industry. The mountain fortifications and the treasure houses remain.

The Goodwins of the Goodwin Sands. The treacherous Goodwin sands, the scene of many disastrous shipwrecks, lie off Kent, a few miles east of Deal, in the Straits of Dover. They extend for about 10 miles and shift unpredictably according to prevailing tides, so that the extensive protective precautions are not always effective. Much of the bank is above water at low tide. The roadstead between the sands and the mainland is known as the Downs.

Local lore claims that they once belonged to the estate of the famous Godwin, the 11th-century Earl of the West Saxons and father of Harold II.

Goodwood of Goodwood. The Sussex racecourse of Goodwood, near Chichester, is famous for its beautiful natural setting and the importance of its racing calendar. It is the seat of the Duke of Richmond and Gordon. Racing has been established there since the opening of the 19th century. The course of the Goodwood Cup is 2 miles 5 furlongs.

There is also a modern course for motor racing, operated by the British Automobile Racing Club.

Gorgonzola of Gorgonzola cheese. The famous rennet cheese, veined and made from the whole milk of cows, is named from its place of origin and continued manufacture. Gorgonzola is a small town in Italy, a few miles north-east of Milan. The cheese is also known as *Stracchino di Gorgonzola*.

The practice of placing layers of hot and cold curd alternately produces cavities in which the whey is retained. This becomes mouldy and yields the characteristic green markings. To accelerate the moulding and to purify the cheese, holes are pierced with a needle. To-day, in the modern factories, the use of selected moulds and Penicillin speeds and simplifies the process.

Goshen of Goshen, a place of light and plenty. The Biblical origin of this allusion is to be found in *Gen. xlvii. 6, 11*, and *Exod. ix. 26*. Goshen was the district in Egypt where Jacob and his family settled. It was "the best of the land" and it escaped the pestilences.

Gotham of the Wise Men of Gotham. The name of the old Nottinghamshire village of Gotham, near the junction of the Trent, is used to describe a notably foolish place. The allusion is to the inhabitants, called the Wise Men of Gotham, who were in fact noted for their stupidity.

Tradition implies that the alleged stupidity was cunningly assumed, to dissuade King John when he visited the place with the intention of buying estates therein.

Gotham gradually became the focus of many stories of fantastic stupidity, such as that of the inhabitants joining hands round a bush to imprison a cuckoo. A wise man of Gotham became the description of a fool, particularly a fantastic fool.

A collection of the *Merrie Tales of the Wise Men of Gotham* appeared in the 16th century. The suspected author was Dr. Andrew Boorde (1490–1549), an English physician who joined the Carthusians, was made suffragan bishop of Chichester and was later released from his monastic vows.

The nomination of a certain district as the focus of a nation's or a district's folly is common throughout the centuries.

In ancient Greece the city of Abdera, on the coast of Thrace, was so designated and its inhabitants were cited as the prototypes of stupidity, despite the fact that the city gave birth to some of the greatest men. They included Protagoras, the sophist, Democritus (known as the Laughing Philosopher in contrast with the melancholy Heraclitus) and Hecatæus, the chronicler and geographer.

New York has been playfully called Gotham in literature and its "Cockney" residents dubbed Gothamites.

Greece of Greek Fire, Cross, Calends, Gift, etc. Greek Fire—the term is still used for a terrifying con-flagration, physical or mental—was a highly combustible material used first by the Greeks of the Byzantine Empire against the Saracens at Constantinople. Its invention is placed in the 7th century and its exact composition is unknown, but it is believed to have contained nitre, sulphur and naphtha. It was used to set fire to ships, fortifications and troops and was used with terrifying and terrible effect. It was claimed that it burned under water.

The Greek Cross corresponds with the St. George's Cross; having equal arms. The Latin Cross has the upright one-third longer than the horizontal cross beam.

The Calends, the first day of the Roman months, were not found in the Greek months, therefore expression "To put off to the Greek Calends" means indefinitely; never.

A Greek gift is a dubious or treacherous gift, deriving from the deceptive Wooden Horse of Troy (*q.v.*).

When Greeks joined Greeks then was the tug
of war,
Philip fought men, but Alexander women.
Nathaniel Lee, *The Rival Queens*, 1677.

The reference is to the Greek resistance to the onslaught of the Macedonian kings, Philip and Alexander. The phrase is still current to describe a struggle between like and equal forces. It is often phrased: "When Greek meets Greek."

For mine own part, it was Greek to me.
Casca, in *Julius Caesar*.

Jonson said of Shakespeare "thou hadst small Latin and less Greek."

The Grecian Bend was a ridiculous, affected method of walking and standing adopted by certain sections of fashionable society towards the end of Queen Victoria's reign. The craze spread to the United States. It was said to derive from Greek postures observed in art.

Greenwich of Greenwich Mean Time, etc. The borough of Greenwich is situated on the south side of the river a few miles from the city of London. It is connected by the Blackwall and other tunnels with the north side.

Greenwich Observatory was erected by Charles II. John Flamsteed (1646–1719) presided and was made the first Astronomer-Royal and installed at Greenwich in 1676. He taught also and was ordained, taking a living in Surrey to supplement his £100 a year salary.

The meridian of Greenwich (longitude 0 in British maps) was accepted as the universal meridian in 1884 at an international conference in Washington. A meridian, or at least a terrestrial meridian, is the line running through that place and through the poles. When the sun passes the meridian of Greenwich it is noon, Greenwich Mean Time, the world standard from which deviations abroad are calculated.

Greenwich Hospital occupies the site of an ancient Royal Palace, known as Greenwich House. It was several times rebuilt and John Evelyn (1620–1706), the diarist, was a commissioner for building it in 1696 when he laid a foundation stone. It was at one time an asylum for disabled seamen and in 1873 became the Royal Naval College, devoted to educational and technical training. The buildings are noted for many examples of Wren's architecture and fine carving and paintings.

At one time sand merchants were known as Greenwich barbers because they were said to shave the local pits to meet the City's demands for sand.

Greenwich was the scene of great fairs on Whit Monday. They became somewhat notorious and the characteristic features were gradually repressed. Dickens (1812–70) refers to them in *Sketches by Boz*: "If the Parks be 'the lungs of London' we wonder what Greenwich Fair is—a periodical breaking out, we suppose— a sort of spring rash."

Last century Greenwich was the site of an annual Whitebait or Fish Dinner, attended by the leading statesmen. It was usually held on the Monday after Trinity.

The Observatory, together with the offices of the Astronomer Royal (established 1675), were removed in 1950 to Hurstmonceaux Castle, near Eastbourne, Sussex. The site provides more adequate accommodation for modern equipment and clearer atmospheric conditions.

Gretna Green of Gretna Green Marriages. The little Scottish village of Gretna Green in Dumfriesshire, near Springfield and 9 miles north-north-west of Carlisle, is just over the border.

It became notorious for clandestine marriages after the abolition of Fleet Marriages (*q.v.*) in the middle of the 18th century.

At that time, in Scotland, all that was required was a declaration before witnesses of a willingness to marry. Gretna Green, among other places, found favour with eloping couples because it was the nearest hamlet where such slight formalities prevailed.

Many were found to exploit the commercial possibilities of the loose restrictions, including one old soldier who, when asked for authority, would declare that he had a special licence from the Government for which he paid £50 a year.

One, Joseph Paisley, did good trade as a so-called blacksmith, but the nearest he had ever been to the trade was forging dubious marriage links. It was said he had been a smuggler and tobacconist.

He used a false or illegible signature and when an action arising from one such marriage compelled him to consult the law, he was advised to retrieve the original certificate and substitute one which recorded him as the witness only of the parties' declaration that they were married.

When the ceremony had been put thus on a more legal basis, or at least a less dangerous one, the "blacksmith" would appear for the marriage in full canonicals. At one time there were rival "ministers" who competed in bribing the postboys to drive the eloping couples to particular establishments.

In 1856 a law was passed that required a three weeks' residence in Scotland by one of the parties.

In recent years the custom has ceased, largely perhaps owing to the greater facilities offered by Register Office marriages.

George Crabbe (1754–1832) wrote a poem entitled *Gretna Green*, which romantic subject has been the theme of many lesser known stories and poems.

Grub Street of Grub Street. According to Dr. Samuel Johnson (1709–84), Grub Street, Moorfields, London, in the ward of Cripplegate, was the place of residence of numerous "writers of small histories, dictionaries, and temporary poems, whence any mean production is called *grubstreet*." The description is from his dictionary entry.

The street was renamed Milton Street in 1830, but the name is said to commemorate a ground landlord, not the famous poet who had many associations with this district between Fore Street and Chiswell Street, Moorfields.

The name grub-street is still applied to collections of hack writers and their productions.

The Grub Street Journal championed the cause of Pope (1688–1744) when his *Dunciad* (1728), which satirized many contemporary figures, produced a violent literary controversy lasting for several years before and after the authorship was openly acknowledged in 1735.

Gruyères of Gruyère cheese. The Swiss town of Gruyères is in the canton of Fribourg, due south of the capital and north-east of the Lake of Geneva. It is famous for its mild, pale-coloured cheese characterized by unusual bubble-like cavities.

Guelders of the Guelder Rose. The *Viburnum Opulus*, or "Snowball Tree," which is much grown in Britain and Europe, is named after the ancient province of Guelders or Gelderland, where it originally flourished.

The province, near the Zuider Zee, was formerly divided between Prussia and the Netherlands. It is a fertile agricultural area.

Guernsey of Guernsey cattle, etc. The second largest of the Channel Island group, Guernsey, is 30 miles from the Normandy coast. It is a centre of intensive agriculture, horticulture, particularly glasshouse products, and exports a valuable granite.

The island's famous breed of cattle, noted for high milk yield, is exported all over the world. It was originally known as the Golden Breed and dates to the 10th century.

A roughly knitted jersey or tunic worn by local sailors and fishermen is also known as a Guernsey. It dates back to Tudor times, when there was a considerable woollen industry in the island. Special wool import facilities were granted by Queen Elizabeth. It is recorded that the Queen bought Guernsey silk-topped stockings and that Mary Stuart wore Guernsey hose at her execution. The Guernsey, only distinguishable by an expert from the Jersey (*q.v.*), was invariably knitted in thick dark blue wool, whereas the Jersey employed other colours and was sometimes of a thinner wool.

The Guildhall of Guildhall. Guildhall is another of the almost generic words of English and particularly London history. It applies to the Guildhall in the City of London, the headquarters or Town Hall of the City Corporation. It is near the Bank of England.

The early City Guilds have been superseded by the Livery Companies, who have their separate Company halls in the City and sustain many historic ceremonies and customs.

The Guildhall, which has been the scene of many historic civic receptions, was severely damaged during the Second World War. It is the City's administrative centre, many courts are held there and the buildings include a notable museum, library and art gallery.

Guinea of Guinea, Guinea fowl, etc. The Guinea coast, of West Africa, which embraces the Gold Coast, Ivory Coast, Sierra Leone, etc., was responsible for the name of the gold coin no longer minted in British currency. It was first struck in Charles the Second's reign, from gold obtained from the Guinea coast. Its value was at first 20s. and it was intended primarily for use in the Guinea trade. The guinea proved popular and was the chief gold coin in this country until it was superseded by the sovereign in 1817. The value of the guinea had fluctuated through the years, but it was legal tender for 21s. from 1717. It was last minted in 1813.

The first designs included an elephant beneath the head of the king on the obverse, an indication of the specialized intention.

Spade guineas were so called because the guineas minted from 1787 for twelve years bore on the reverse a spade-shaped shield—like the spade of the playing card—carrying the royal arms and inscriptions.

The popularity of the coin is evident in its survival in professional, club and other fees, though there is no current coin of the value of 21s.

This application of the term accounts for the phrase "a guinea pig." It is applied, in a derogatory sense, to professional men more concerned with the guineas than with their work, to directors who often sat on numerous boards and collected fees in guineas without always earning them, or lent their name to encourage share applications, to "supply" clergymen whose fee for a Sunday's duties was often a guinea.

The Guinea fowl was introduced from the Guinea coast.

The Guinea, or Cavy, pig is a South American rodent and the name is not thought to have any connection with the Guinea coast.

Gulf of Mexico of the Gulf Stream. Many who refer to the Gulf Stream, which passes the shores of Britain, have no knowledge of the Gulf concerned. It is the Gulf of Mexico, whence the stream passes along the east coast of the United States. It is joined by a second current from the West Indies, and when it enters the Atlantic it is more properly called the Gulf Stream Drift. It divides, flowing north and south. It has a modifying effect upon the climate of western Europe. Its passage varies with the seasons and tropical fish, brought in its waters, have been found as far as 20 miles from the Gulf Stream's normal channel.

Hackney of Hackney carriage, Hack, etc. Many centuries ago the term hack, or hackney, was applied to ordinary workaday horses, used for casual riding as opposed to military purposes.

The use is still applied in the words "hack" and "hacking." Later the name was given to horses let out for hire and to horse-drawn vehicles similarly employed. The original Hackney coach was a two-horse vehicle, often one discarded by the nobility and declining to public hire.

Hackney, the north-eastern metropolitan borough of London, is associated by many with the origin of the name. It was held to be the starting-place of many Hackney carriages, and the fields of the district were noted as the collecting ground for the horses to be sold at the great Smithfield Horse Fairs.

A survival of this association is seen in the name Mare Street for part of the thoroughfare from Hackney to Smithfield.

Ivor Brown, in *Having the Last Word*, prefers the derivation from *haquenée*, the saddle mare of the French ladies.

The word, in its connotation of "workaday, ordinary," is seen in the hack writer, the hackneyed expression, etc.

Hamburg of Hamburgh grape and fowl. The German city and port of Hamburg, on the Elbe, is responsible for the name of the locally grown grape, the Hamburgh, which is extensively marketed and sometimes listed as Hambro.

The city also gave its name to the type of domestic fowl.

Hameln of the Pied Piper of Hamelin. The German town of Hameln,

south-south-west of Hanover, is the scene of the ancient legend immortalized by Robert Browning (1812–89) in *The Pied Piper of Hamelin*. This "Child's Story" is included in his *Dramatic Romances*, 1845.

The legend is set varyingly in the 13th and 14th centuries, when the burghers were said to be distraught by the plague of rats which threatened the health and livelihood of the town.

There appeared an ancient musician in a fantastical coat of many colours who claimed that by means of the seduction of his shrill pipe he could rid the town of the vermin. He was known as the Pied Piper, and the burghers readily agreed to the man's terms.

The Pied Piper thereon went through the streets playing and the rats swarmed after him until he led them into the river of Hameln, the Weser, and they were drowned.

The city fathers, who had bargained sceptically and with little hope of success, now refused to honour their agreement and the stranger, in revenge, piped again through the streets of Hameln. This time the children of the place swarmed after him, out of the gates of the city and to a little hill, the side of which opened and the Piper and his train disappeared therein. Varying accounts say that a lame boy and a blind child lagging, did not disappear but returned to tell the tale. The children vanished and the men of the town searched for them in vain. They are said not to have perished but to have been led by the Piper to Transylvania where they founded a German colony.

The belief that rats can be charmed away by music or rhyme persisted in the folklore of several countries.

Out of the houses rats came tumbling—
Great rats, small rats, lean rats, brawny rats

Brown rats, black rats, grey rats, tawny rats,
And step by step they followed him dancing,
Till they came to the river Weser.

The Pied Piper of Hamelin.

Harris of Harris tweed.

The district of Harris occupies the southern part of the island of Lewis in the Outer Hebrides, Inverness-shire, Scotland. Harris also embraces some of the smaller islands separated from it in the south by the Sound of Harris, and St. Kilda, widely separated on the west. The inhabitants of Harris, engaged in fishing, sheep farming and crofting, or the working of small holdings, weave the famous Harris tweeds on hand looms. They are noted for their durability.

The word Tweed is not directly derived from the district. It is claimed that a London merchant read as "tweed" an ill-written "tweel," which referred to twi- or two-patterned nature of the material.

Hatton Garden of Hatton Garden.

The Holborn, London, street of Hatton Garden is synonymous with the diamond and allied trades. Merchants and allied traders still occupy most of its offices and deals in precious stones are still transacted extensively in its streets and cafés.

It was named after Sir Christopher Hatton, "the Dancing Chancellor," a favourite of Queen Elizabeth. Among the royal favours bestowed upon him was, during a vacancy in the see, Ely Palace, Holborn, the province of the Bishop of Ely. It had a remarkable garden, to which Shakespeare makes reference in *Richard III, iii. 4.*

A later occupant of the see of Ely, Matthew Wren, uncle of the architect, made unsuccessful efforts to recover his garden from Hatton's widow.

Havana of Havana.

The capital of Cuba, Havana, a university city, maritime and air port, is noted for its tobacco industry. Its famous cigars have made the city's name synonymous with the product and a symbol of quality.

Hawthornden of "Drummond of Hawthornden."

William Drummond (1585–1649), the Scottish poet, pamphleteer and hymnologist, has, by his title, brought into literature a name that few could place. His "sweet and solitary seat," Hawthornden, was a few miles north of Edinburgh. His father, Sir John, was Laird of Hawthornden.

Drummond, a friend of Michael Drayton, depends much for his notice, if not for his fame, upon the visit paid to him by the Poet Laureate, Ben Jonson. After studying law and literature at Edinburgh and abroad Drummond lived almost a recluse. He produced sonnets inspired by the early death of his first love which caused him to be called "The Scottish Petrarch."

Jonson's journey to Scotland, in 1618, when he was supreme and, incidentally, a sedentary man weighing nearly 20 stone, was not prompted by a visit to Drummond, of whom he knew little. Jonson was given the Freedom of Edinburgh and later a civic banquet. The reason for the stay at Hawthornden is not established, but the records which Drummond kept of the conversations provide information about the visitor and contemporary personalities. The manuscript was lost among numerous papers at Hawthornden for nearly a century after the author's death.

Mount Helicon of Helicon, Heliconian.

The use of the words Helicon and Heliconian to denote a source of poetic inspiration or association derives from Mount Helicon, in fact a range of mountains in Bœotia, in ancient Greece, near the Gulf of Corinth.

It was held to be the abode of the Muses and sacred to them. The fountains of Aganippe and Hippocrene were there, connected by Helicon's stream.

The allusion is frequently found in literature.

Helos of Helot. A helot, a slave or serf, is probably so called from the town of Helos, in Laconia in ancient Greece. Other authorities suggest that the name derived from the Greek word for capture.

The Serfs of Sparta were known as helots. They had no political or civic rights and were held in rigid subjection. Many worked on the land, allocated to particular citizens. Occasionally they served as emergency troops.

Helston of the Helston Furry, or Floral Dance. Helston, the Cornish borough and market town, received its first Charter in 1201. It is world-famous for its annual Furry, or Floral Dance, held on May 8, the Feast of the Apparition of St. Michael, the Archangel, who is patron saint of Helston. The parish church is mentioned as dedicated to St. Michael as early as 1208. The Manor of Helston was given by William the Conqueror to his half-brother, the Count of Mortain, whose patron saint was St. Michael. The archangel, slaying the dragon, is the design of the Borough seal.

The old spring festival had religious origins, springing from pagan rites, and similar ceremonies were in early centuries held elsewhere in Cornwall, but they have not survived.

The name, Furry, derives from the ancient Cornish word *fer*, a fair or festivity, and perhaps from the Latin *feria*, which originally implied a holy day.

The story current last century that the celebration marks a conflict between Michael and the devil for possession of the town was based on the then current supposition that Helston was a corruption of Hell's stone or Hell's town. In fact, the records prove that the early name of the town was Henliston, the old court town.

Helston is decorated with flower for the annual ceremony and th dancers, originally drawn from th staffs of the large houses, follow a se circuit. The revels, accompanied b music, are joined by the spectators

By ancient tradition the first tw couples should be Helston born anc buttonholes of lilies of the valle should be worn. There is a tradi tional dance tune and measure anc a Furry song entitled the Hal-an-Tow in which the last word rhymes witl "now."

Nowadays a Horse Show distract attention from the Dance itself.

The popular ballad, *The Flora Dance*, was written by Katie Moss.

Henley of Henley Regatta. Th term "Henley," almost synonymou with rowing, has its origin in th Roman town of Henley-on-Thames Oxfordshire. Its world-famous ama teur regatta was founded in 1839 The Royal four-day event include such famous awards as the Grand Challenge Cup for Eight Oars Ladies' Challenge Plate for Eigh Oars (1845); Thames Challenge Cup for Eight Oars (1868); Stewards' Cur for Four Oars (1841); Visitors' Chal lenge Cup for Four Oars (1847) Wyfold Cup for Four Oars (1855) Goblets and Nickalls' Cup for Pai Oars (1845); Diamond Sculls (1844)

The Head of the River Champion ship (1925) and Olympic contests arc also held at Henley, which is the "Lord's" of rowing.

The Grand Challenge Cup is the highest rowing award in the world and attracts international entries.

The first Oxford and Cambridge Boat Race was held at Henley in 1829.

The town supports ancillary industries, also malting and brewing, and is a residential town for London workers.

Hesse of Hessian. The coarse, strong fabric known as hessian, and made from hemp or jute, takes its name from the west German republic of Hesse. The material is much used in the Services.

Hesse, which is watered by the Rhine, is largely an agricultural area, with woodlands and vineyards. Hemp, flax and tobacco are among the main crops.

A high boot, first worn by troops in the area, was called a Hessian boot and there is a Hessian fly which causes great damage to cereal crops. Its unusual cocoon is known as a flax seed.

Hess's Law, in chemistry, derives not from Germany but from the 19th-century Russian chemist, G. H. Hess.

Hocheim of Hock. The village of Hocheim, of which the name Hock is a contraction, is situated in the former Prussian province of Hessen, between Mainz, or Mayence, and Frankfurt. Its vineyards produced the true hock, but now the name is applied to wine grown on the banks of the Rhine or its tributaries, between Coblenz and Mannheim, and in the former Bavarian Palatinate. Hock, popularly regarded as a white wine, may in fact be white or red, and still or sparkling. Its characteristic bottles are brick or orange coloured.

Holland of Holland, Hollandaise. The coarse, tough linen known as Holland, was formerly manufactured in Holland. It is often sold unbleached and of a brown colour. The original Holland, which took the name of its place of manufacture, was of a much finer texture. It was known as Holland cloth.

Hollandaise, in cookery, implies in the Dutch style and is the name of a notable sauce, served with fish and certain vegetables.

Hollywood of Hollywood. The name Hollywood is a world synonym for the U.S. film industry. The Californian centre was annexed to Los Angeles in 1910. It offered ample land for development, constant sunshine and magnificent panoramic scenery, when the film industry was in its infancy at the beginning of this century.

The word Hollywood is also used in an adjectival sense to characterize the vast expenditure, opulent production and general magnificent showmanship that is typical of the U.S. film industry.

Homburg vor der Höhe of the Homburg hat. The Prussian spa of Homburg vor der Höhe, near Frankfort, claims to have been the place where the men's soft felt hat, with a dented crown, was worn. The name Homburg was general in Britain until it was partially displaced by the appellation "Trilby," from George du Maurier's best seller of that name, published in 1894. The fashion was superseded between the two World Wars by the similar shaped hat in black felt, called the "Anthony Eden," owing to the Foreign Secretary's apparent preference for it.

Huntingdon of the Countess of Huntingdon's Connection. The trustees of the Countess of Huntingdon's Connection still have their central offices, though most of their places of worship are now affiliated with the Congregational Union. They record between thirty and forty chapels and stations at the present time.

The association with the inland county of Huntingdonshire is through Selina Hastings (1707–91), who married the 9th Earl of Huntingdon. She was converted by her sister to Methodism and thenceforward devoted her life and means to religious works. She was a close associate of John and Charles Wesley and of George Whitefield. She erected several chapels, the first at Brighton in 1761. One of her particular aims was to enlist the sympathy and labours of the monied classes. For that reason several of her original chapels were founded at fashionable spas. She established a religious training college for the propagation of her views and extended her work to the United States.

Hurlingham of Hurlingham.

Although interest in this country in polo has waned somewhat of recent years, Hurlingham is still the name instantly thought of as epitomizing this sport.

Hurlingham Park is at Fulham, London, and polo, extensively played abroad, particularly in Service circles, owes its recognition in Britain to its adoption by the Hurlingham Club in 1873. The Westchester Cup, contested by England and the U.S.A., and the Oxford and Cambridge Contests are two of the leading events in the sport in this country.

The other leading clubs are at Ranelagh and Roehampton.

Meadow Brook, where the game was first played in 1879, is the United States equivalent of Hurlingham.

Kipling (1865–1936) has extensive descriptions of polo in his story *The Maltese Cat*, published in a collection of stories entitled *The Day's Work* in 1898.

Hyde Park of Hyde Park, Hyde Park Orators.

The famous park, situated in the west end of London, between Piccadilly and Kensington, originally belonged to the Manor of Hyde, under the jurisdiction of the Abbey at Westminster. It occupies nearly 400 acres and is world famous for many contrasting features. They include the Marble Arch, now separated from it, the fashionable Park Lane which flanks it, the Serpentine, Hyde Park Corner, and the "Spouters'

Corner," near the Marble Arch, where open-air speakers on all subjects and of all degrees of eloquence and erudition hold forth to whatever audiences they can collect by their subject, sincerity or eccentricity.

Here may be seen a tonsured monk, a violent political agitator, a rescue worker or a racing tipster. The rostrums are portable stands or boxes and large crowds gather to be instructed, to be obstructive or to be merely amused.

A generous measure of latitude is allowed by an indulgent but perspicacious police force. A classic story, apocryphal perhaps, but typical, is of the foreigner who stopped his car to listen and heard a Hyde Park orator denouncing the Royal Family. The listener rushed to the nearest policeman to report the infamy, only to be told that the orator was harmless but that the reporting motorist would be well advised not to stop there with his engine running as he might cause a public nuisance.

Hyde Park was for centuries a fashionable parade ground and as such is mentioned frequently in literature, particularly in the Restoration plays, etc.

> *Beyond Hyde Park all is a desert.*
> *The Man of Mode* (1676).

> *Ay, we'll all walk in the park; the ladies talked of being there.*
> *The Way of the World*, Congreve (1700).

James Shirley (1596–1666) wrote a comedy entitled *Hyde Park*, presented in 1632 to mark the opening of the Park to the public, and subsequently printed. It is a notable record of contemporary modes and manners.

Ilium of the Iliad. Troy (*q.v.*), the ancient city on the Asiatic shore of the Hellespont, was reputed to be founded by Ilus, and in consequence named Ilium, or Ilion.

The *Iliad*, the great epic poem attributed to Homer (between 12th and 9th centuries B.C.), is devoted to the war against Troy waged by the Achæan princes to recover Helen, wife of Menelaus, whom Paris, son of the king of Troy, had carried back to the city.

Paris, whose destruction had been attempted as a child because the soothsayers foretold that he would bring disaster upon his country, was appointed judge of the relative charms of Hera, Aphrodite and Athene. Aphrodite's lure is the promise of the fairest wife in the world. Paris awards her the prize and persuades the lovely Helen to elope with him to Troy.

The *Iliad* is in twenty-four books, perhaps an arbitrary division resulting from the original distribution on the same number of rolls of papyrus.

The wrath of Achilles, arising from an insult from Agamemnon, the Greek leader at the siege of Troy, is one of the main themes of the *Iliad* and prompted the lines by Dr. John Wolcot (Peter Pindar, 1738–1819):

What had Achilles been without his Homer?
A tailor, woollen-draper, or a comber!

The term "Iliad" is used to describe a sequence of misfortunes or woes.

India of Indian file, Indian summer, etc. The word India survives in many terms not now, and in some cases never, specifically associated with the country.

Indian file, or single line progress, is named from the habit of the American Indians who tracked one behind the other, stepping in each other's footsteps and the last man obliterating the trail, thus rendering detection and estimation of approaching numbers difficult.

The Red Indians were the aboriginal race of North America.

Indian Summer is the term applied to a mild spell which frequently occurs in this country at the end of October, and is common on the Atlantic coasts and central States of the U.S.A. Sometimes the fine period, which in America often produces forest fires, occurs as late as November or December.

The noticeable fine period is sometimes referred to in Britain as St. Luke's Summer or St. Martin's Summer from the days of these two saints on October 18 and November 11 respectively.

Except St. Martin's summer, halcyon days.
I Henry VI. i. 2.

India paper, used for proofs of engravings, was primarily imported from China. There is also a very thin, tough printing paper so called, used for compact editions of books.

Indian ink comes from China and Japan.

Indian corn, or maize, is a native of the Americas. It is used as fodder, for meal and breadmaking and for producing maize beer.

The bottle-shaped Indian club, used in gymnasia, was frequently found in Indian athletic events.

The nasturtium is known as Indian cress and the true nasturtium is in fact the watercress. The garden flowers incorrectly called nasturtiums are species of *Tropæolum*.

The Indian fig is the banyan tree, or *Ficus indica*, in which group the indiarubber tree is included. The Banyan is a sacred tree in many parts of India. Its roots hang downwards from the branches, forming a palisade.

Indian hemp, or Bhang, is used in

many forms as an intoxicant and narcotic. Taken in excess it produces deleterious effects similar to those associated with opium.

India House was the headquarters of the old East India Company, in Leadenhall Street, London. It is noted in literature through the writings of Charles Lamb (1775–1834), who was employed there from 1792 to 1825.

Ionia of Ionian, Ionic. Ionia was a district of the west coast of Asia Minor, near Smyrna, and including the adjacent islands in the Ægean Sea. Smyrna is the Izmir of modern Turkey.

It was a region prominent in the early development of ancient Greek philosophy and literature. The Ionians were one of the ancient tribes of Greece.

. The Ionian Mode in music is applied to an ancient Greek form distinguished by a certain effeminacy. The Ionic dialect was one of the four forms of the Greek language. The Ionic Order of architecture, of which the famous temple of Diana at Ephesus was a classic example, is distinguished by two lateral volutes of the capital of the pillar.

Ireland of Irish Bull. The Irish bull, or Irishism, for the blunder or contradiction, usually verbal, is fathered on Ireland only because Irish folk are said to make such statements more frequently and more colourfully than the people of other nations.

Irish stew is thought to be so named from the preponderance in the recipe of potatoes, which are extensively grown and eaten in Ireland.

Irish moss, or carrageen, is an edible seaweed found on European and North American rocky shores. When boiled, after drying and bleaching, it yields a pleasant drink or jelly. It is frequently recommended by medical men. The moss is also used as fodder and as a dry stuffing for domestic goods.

The Irish terrier, one of the larger terriers, came into prominence as an accepted breed about 1870. It is noted for its pluck and even temper. The Irish wolfhound, originally used in hunting wolves, is an ancient breed which became almost extinct towards the end of last century, but was revived. Some are still used for their original purpose in Canada and the United States. The Irish setter is one of the oldest recorded breeds of setter. It is an expert gun dog.

Izmir of Izimir. The flourishing city and port of Smyrna, now renamed Izmir, on the west coast of Turkey, has given its name to one of the chief wine exports of the country.

For centuries Turkey has been famous for its vineyards and indeed it is claimed that it was from a navigator of Foca, on the west coast, that France derived her national wines and her world-famous export. Homer praised the Phrygian vineyards of Turkey in 900 B.C.

Until comparatively recently the wines of Turkey were never offered to the outside world, owing to religious restrictions. Now the markets are becoming world-wide and Izmir and Tekirdag (Tekirdag, formerly Rodosto, is a town on the Sea of Marmora) are two notable white table wines. The Turkish liqueur, Mersin, from Mersina, a port north-north-east of Cyprus, is a triple sec white curaçao (*q.v.*), which offers the aromatic flavour of the local oranges.

Jagannathi of Jaconet. The substantial cotton cloth, frequently waterproofed and used for poulticing, etc., is named jaconet from the Bengal town of Jagannathi, where it was originally manufactured. The town was also known as Juggernaut (*q.v.*) or Puri. It is a sacred town of the Hindus and a place of pilgrimages.

Jaffa of the Jaffa orange. The ancient Palestinian town of Jaffa is now linked with modern Tel Aviv. It is some 50 miles north-west of Jerusalem of which it was in ancient days the port.
  The characteristic local orange is a leading export.
  Jaffa is the ancient city of Joppa and was the chief seaport of Judea. It is mentioned frequently in the Bible and is the port at which were landed the cedars brought for the building of Solomon's temple (*2 Chron. ii. 16*).

Jalapa of Jalap. Jalap, commonly corrupted in the Services and elsewhere to "jollop," is a well-known purgative derived from the dried root of a plant in the convolvulus family.
  It is a native of Mexico and takes its name from the town of Jalapa, Vera Cruz, where it grows at high altitudes. The root, which contains sugar, starch and other ingredients, yields a resin which, when extracted with alcohol, is the basis of the widely used medicinal powder.

Japan or Japanning. The Japanese empire gave its name to a hard varnish and its application to wood, metal, stone, etc., which originated there and has since been extensively employed by many countries. The term, originally applied to notable lacquering, is now applicable to less skilled and less artistic developments of the baked varnish process.
  The name Japan is also seen in Japanese lanterns, and in Japanese vellum, a costly hand-made paper manufactured from the inner lining of the bark of the mulberry tree. It is also reflected in the plant and tree name, *japonica*.

Jericho of "Go to Jericho," etc. This and similar expressions, such as "I wish you at Jericho," are intimations, in varying degrees of offensiveness, that the person may go as far away as possible—and stop as long as he or she likes. The phrase "He's gone to Jericho" implies that the person has gone to an unknown destination, and the speaker cares little where it is. The origin of the town name in such phrases probably derives from the Biblical reference: "And the king said, Tarry at Jerusalem until your beards be grown, and then return," to be found in *2 Sam. x. 5*, and *1 Chron. xix. 5*.
  Timbuktu (*q.v.*) is cited in a similar fashion.

Jersey of Jersey, Jersey cows, cabbages. The largest of the Channel Island group, Jersey, lies about 15 miles from the Normandy coast. It has given its name to the close-fitting woollen garment which is worn by the island's fishermen and farm-workers, as it is worn by their counterparts in many countries of the world. In Tudor times there was a considerable knitting industry in the island and special import licences for wool were granted by Queen Elizabeth. Woollen garments were also supplied to the mariners attracted by the trade with Newfoundland which Raleigh fostered when Governor of Jersey from 1600–3. There is little to distinguish the Jersey from other woollen garments so named, except that originally it was knitted in a special stitch, known in the Jersey patois as *ouvre*.

Jersey cows, among the most famous and most carefully preserved strains in the world, are small, prolific milk-yielders of a pleasing fawn colour.

Jersey cabbages, a favourite attraction with tourists, are a local variety which grows to a height of six or more feet. The stalks, when dried, are made into sturdy walking-sticks.

The Jersey lily, of doubtful original association with the island, is pink and leafless.

Jodhpur of Jodhpurs. The familiar riding habits of long breeches, close fitting from knee to ankle, are called Jodhpurs from the state and capital of that name in Rajputana, India. It is an arid region, bordering on the Indian desert and the alternative name, Marwar, reflects this for it means region of death.

The capital is fortified and guards the Maharajah's palace.

There is a textile industry, chiefly cotton, and some mining and metal manufacture.

The normal attire for Indians is the *paijama*, silk or cotton baggy trousers, and these, though cool, are not suitable for riding.

During the 19th century a Maharajah of Jodhpur ordered his tailor to devise some form of riding attire which combined the serviceability of breeches and boots with the coolness and comfort of the *paijama*. The tailor at length produced the hybrid garment since known as jodhpurs.

The skill of the native tailors in making jodhpurs is still unsurpassed, but the art is not confined to Jodhpur. The garments of many of the ruling Princes are to-day made in Meerut.

Jordan of Jordan, "Jordan passed." The jordan was a recognized and widely used type of bottle in medicine and science several centuries ago. Its name is thought to have derived from similarity of shape with the characteristic flask sold to pilgrims who brought back water from the river Jordan. The name later passed vulgarly to the domestic chamber.

"Jordan passed," a phrase familiar in religious writing and hymnology, implied death, an allusion to the arbitrary division, by the river Jordan, of the wilderness of the world and the Promised Land. In a sense Jordan was the Christian counterpart of the Styx of the ancients. It is the chief river of Palestine and has a notable place in the Old and New Testaments. It was the Jordan which divided so that the Israelites passed over on dry land (*Joshua iii. 16–17*), and it was in the Jordan that Christ was baptized by John the Baptist (*Mark i. 5–9*).

Jordan almonds, a variety of fine quality, have no association with the Jordan of Palestine. They are grown chiefly in Spain and the name is a corruption of the French *jardin*, garden.

Juggernaut of Juggernaut. The Bengal town of Juggernaut, Jagannathi (see *Jaconet*), or Puri, is capital of the district of the same name. It stands on the west coast of the Bay of Bengal.

It is a holy place of the Hindus, housing a temple sacred to Krishna, the eighth and final incarnation, or avatar, of Vishnu, the man-god or god-man, known as Jagannatha, lord of the world.

At annual festivals, which attract thousands of pilgrims, the idol of the god is paraded on a huge decorated car. In earlier times pilgrims are said to have thrown themselves under the wheels of the great car, thus securing a holy death. This association prompts the use of the word juggernaut for an object or movement to which people blindly sacrifice themselves. It is probable, however, that the deaths were inevitable casualties due to the press and fervour of the occasion.

K

Kent of Kentish Men, Men of Kent, Kentish Fire, etc. Kent, the south-eastern promontory county, known as the Garden of England, is famous for its fruit and hop gardens, for Canterbury (*q.v.*), with its Mother-Church of England (the seat of St. Augustine, Thomas à Becket and other great archbishops), for the Cinque ports of Hastings, Sandwich, Romney, Hythe and Dover. The latter, like Folkestone, is a great Channel port.

The county gives its name to the Kentish Codling apple and other local fruit varieties.

Men of Kent are those born east of the Medway, the county's dividing river; Kentish men are those born to the west of the Medway.

"Kent, sir—everybody knows Kent—apples,
cherries, hops, and women."
Pickwick Papers, Chapter 2.

Kent, in the commentaries of Caesar writ,
Is termed the civillest place of all this isle.
2 Henry VI. iv. 7.

Kentish Fire is a term applied to vehement applause, measured, accented, in unison and often accompanied by stamping. It is thought to have arisen from its use in Kent during the protests against the Roman Catholic emancipation movement (1818–29). The system of applause, sometimes serving as an interruption, has become associated with religious protest meetings and in this connection was much utilized in Irish meetings and demonstrations.

Kentish Rag is the name given to local limestone, of a greyish-blue colour, found on the coasts of the county.

The Fair Maid of Kent, whose beauty earned her the title, was Joan, Countess of Salisbury, who, after two previous marriages, became wife of the Black Prince (1330–76), her cousin. She was the only daughter of the Earl of Kent. Recent scientific examination of the tomb of the Black Prince in Canterbury Cathedral has proved that his armour, claimed by some to have given rise to the title, was not so coloured.

The Holy Maid of Kent was Elizabeth Barton (16th century), who believed she was inspired, and was certainly exploited, to stir up resistance to the Reformation. She, a serving maid, became a nun at Canterbury. She not only opposed Henry VIII's divorce to facilitate his marriage with Anne Boleyn, but she publicly predicted his speedy death as a result of his action.

She was arrested and executed at Tyburn in 1534, having been found guilty of a charge of high treason.

Kentucky of Kentucky Minstrels. The connection between the southern central state of Kentucky with the familiar minstrel troupe, appears to have been largely due to the famous song writer, Stephen Foster (1826–64).

Kentucky, a tobacco and cereal producing state, includes the famous "blue-grass" regions. Coal is mined, cattle reared and petroleum is an important product. The picturesque Kentucky river, running through deep limestone chasms and traversed in parts by pleasure steamers, enters the Ohio river.

Kentucky was originally a part of Virginia.

Stephen Foster was noted for his negro melodies and with his consent E. P. Christy was at first assumed to be author and composer of the famous *Swanee River* or *The Old Folks at Home* (1851). Christy's famous minstrel troupe made this and other Foster songs famous throughout the United States and in Great Britain.

The term Kentucky Minstrels has since implied a coloured troupe and the Kentucky Minstrels of British broadcasting were formed in 1933 by Harry S. Pepper. Many famous modern songs were composed specially for the Minstrels.

A Kentucky boat, an ark-like flat craft, about 40 ft. long, was characteristic of the district and is mentioned frequently in U.S. literature.

A Kentucky pill was a local name for a bullet and a Kentucky bite was a familiar sporting term for a wrestling hold.

Kerry of the Kerry Blue Terrier. The Irish county of Kerry supported the breed of large terrier known as the Kerry Blue, chiefly for use among hill cattle and pigs. The spirited strain is also used for badgers. In this country, where it has been recognized and popularized since 1922, it is favoured trimmed.

Kerry, a maritime county in southwest Eire, is an agricultural area, with a considerable fishing industry. The county contains the famous Tralee (the capital), Killarney's lakes, and the Macgillicuddy Reeks, the highest Irish range.

Kidderminster of Kidderminster carpets. The Worcestershire town of Kidderminster, 14 miles north of the county town and cathedral city, has been famous for over 200 years for the manufacture of carpets. Originally the pattern was achieved by the intersection of cloths of differing colours or shades. The carpets are not as extensively made nowadays and other varieties have rivalled them. The characteristic flat type of carpet, with no pile and the pattern in reverse on the back, was also made in Scotland.

The town also supports mills, dye works and tin plate and allied industries.

Kilkenny of "To fight like Kilkenny cats." The expression "to fight like Kilkenny cats" implies desperate destruction until all is lost by both sides.

Kilkenny is a county in Eire, flanked on the west by Tipperary and on the east by Co. Carlow and Co. Wexford. The capital, Kilkenny, is on the Nore and offers an ancient cathedral and ruins of Dominican and Franciscan monasteries.

The association of the city with the phrase is said to have arisen from an incident during the Irish rebellion of 1798 when a foreign garrison started the cruel diversion of tying two cats together by their tails and throwing them across a line to fight it out. On the approach of authority a soldier is said to have cut off the tails with his sword, when the cats made off. His story when challenged was that two cats had been fighting and the tails were all that was left of them.

The allusion gained endorsement in subsequent years when the contentions between the two halves of the capital were carried to such lengths—and depths—that they threatened to ruin both.

Kilkenny supports cattle and crops, and anthracite is mined.

Kola of Kolinsky. The fur of the Siberian mink, known as Kolinsky, is named from the district of production, Kola, in Russian Lapland. The town of Kola is near Murmansk, famous during the Second World War, and was itself an Allied depot during the First World War. The district, which is north of the Arctic Circle, is chiefly concerned in fishing.

The mink is a small, semi-aquatic animal of the weasel or stoat type. In cold climates it produces a thick fur of varying shades of brown.

The Kremlin of the Kremlin. The Kremlin, which is synonymous to the outside world with the highest official opinion of Soviet Russia, is apt to be thought of as a product of the Revolution, since when it has assumed international significance.

In fact it is an ancient citadel or

fortress around which Moscow has grown for centuries. For an equally long period it has been the centre of Russian political and religious life. Within its walls are the Czars' palaces, great historic churches and palaces of the nobles. The famous Red Square, scene of great political and military demonstrations, is at the walls of the Kremlin whose buildings are now occupied by Soviet officials and ministries.

In the 17th century an Englishman erected the famous peal of bells above the Kremlin gate on which are now played *The Internationale* and other tunes with which the donor would have been unfamiliar.

L

Labrador of the Labrador Retriever. The peninsula of Labrador is situated between the Hudson Bay and the Gulf of St. Lawrence, in the east of the North American continent. It was named by a Portuguese navigator, Cortereal, from the Portuguese word *llavrador*, a yeoman farmer.

It was ceded to Great Britain in 1763. It is flanked on the west by Quebec and is separated from Newfoundland by the Strait of Belle Isle. Sir Wilfred Grenfell, the British medical missionary (b. 1865), is inseparably associated with Labrador in whose development and welfare he played a magnificent part. He made the world conscious of the country and its maritime people.

The Labrador retriever has been known in this country for nearly 200 years and is thought to have been introduced by the fishing and lumber crews from Labrador who visited English ports. The black labrador is a successful field and show dog and much sought as a companion. The Golden, or Yellow, Labrador is less noted in the field. Its colour is thought to derive from the Chesapeake (*q.v.*) strain.

Laconia of Laconic. The word Laconic, denoting a pithy and concise approach, derives from Laconia or Laconica, a State in the southeast of the Peloponnese founded by the Dorians. The capital was Sparta. The inhabitants of Sparta (*spartan* implies endurance and simplicity) were noted for their pithy speech. When the ruler received from Philip of Macedon the advice "If I enter Laconia, I will level Lacedaemon to the ground" they replied "If."

Caesar's *Veni, vidi, vici* is an example of the laconism or the laconic style. Victor Hugo (1802–85), anxious as to the reception of a new book, is said to have sent to his publishers a postcard bearing only the sign "?" The publishers replied "!"

The word was earlier spelt laconick.

Landau of Landau and Landaulet. The four-wheeled carriage, with front and back top halves that can be raised and lowered independently, was first made in Landau, in Bavaria, in the 18th century. It is an historic, once fortified town, and was prominent in the Thirty Years War. The association survives in landaulet, which is a coupé with a landau roof.

Land's End of Land's End to John o' Groats. Land's End, the south-west promontory of Cornwall, is the most westerly point of the British Isles. It consists of rough, caved, granite cliffs with an Atlantic outcrop of dangerous rocks marked by the Longships Lighthouse.

The expression "from Land's End to John o' Groats" grew naturally from the linking of the extremities of the kingdom. Burns (1759–96) wrote:

> *Frae Maidenkirk to Johnny Groat's . . .*
> *A chield's amang you takin' notes.*

Tradition says that Jan Groot came from Holland in the reign of James IV of Scotland (1488–1513) and purchased lands on the north-east tip of the country.

He flourished so that at one time there were eight families bearing the name. Annually they met in the house of their founder and there, on one occasion, pride confused the question of precedence. The patriarch promised to prevent a recurrence of the dispute. He built an octagonal room with eight doors and placed therein an octagonal table so that each branch of the family should meet on an equality.

The site of the house was near Duncansby Head.

Laodicea of Laodicean.

In the Roman province of Phrygia, Asia Minor, Laodicea was a city of importance and wealth. It was situated in the valley of the Mæander (*q.v.*). Eventually it became an episcopal see, but in the first days of Christianity the inhabitants were lukewarm and half-hearted, so that the term persists to this day to describe such characteristics.

St. John wrote to them: ". . . thou art neither cold nor hot: I would thou wert cold or hot. So then because thou art lukewarm, and neither cold nor hot, I will spue thee out of my mouth" (*Rev. iii. 15–16*).

Thomas Hardy (1840–1928) used the title, *The Laodicean*, for a novel published in 1881.

Laon of Lawn.

The French city of Laon, in the department of Aisne, gives its name to the fine linen known as lawn and particularly associated in this country with the material used for the vestment of a bishop or archbishop, known as a rochet. Prelates were at one time frequently referred to as "Men of lawn."

The material is named in *The Winter's Tale, iv. 3*, and Francis Quarles (1592–1644), refers to:

Lawn sleeves and rochets shall go down,
And hey! then up go we!

The linen factories of Laon are now less numerous and prominent.

In earlier days the use of the Edinburgh lawn market as a place of executions led to the adoption of the phrase, "Going to the lawn market," as a synonym for the death sentence or its consequences.

Latakia of Latakia.

The ancient city of Laodicea (*q.v.*), in Phrygia, Asia Minor, is now the Syrian port of Latakia, due east of Cyprus. Tobacco is one of its chief exports and the port has given its name to the pro-

duct that is used very extensively in tobacco mixtures.

Lebanon of the Cedar of Lebanon.

The lofty mountain range of Lebanon, in Syria, is widely known through the frequent Old Testament references to its cedar forests. Its trees supplied fine timber for the temple and palace of Solomon. The district was also noted for its wine (*Hos. xiv. 7*). The Lebanon cedar is associated geographically with the Mount Atlas Cedar and the Deodar. The magnificent tree, with its curving, almost horizontal branches, is used in this country primarily for decorative purposes. The timber, when grown in Britain, is not of outstanding quality. As the species is not mentioned in Evelyn's *Silva* (1664) it is presumed not to have been grown extensively in this country before that date.

The cedars, which were spoken of as "the glory of Lebanon," and were used as a figure of speech by the psalmist and others, were said to have been introduced into France by two seeds given to the botanist de Jussieu by the authorities of Kew in the middle of the 18th century.

Leghorn of Leghorn straw, poultry.

The chief seaport of Tuscany, in Northern Italy, Leghorn (Ital. *Livorno*) is due north of Elba. It is a popular resort and has extensive harbours. Its 17th-century cathedral has an unexpected feature in a façade designed by the English architect, Inigo Jones (1573–1652).

Leghorn straw and hats made therefrom are one of the chief exports. There is also a large trade in oils, silk, coral, wines, etc. The name is seen also in breeds of poultry originally associated with the city.

Lesbos of Lesbian.

The large Ægean island of Lesbos, in the Greek peninsula, off the coast of Asia Minor, is now known as Mitylene, which was the name of its former capital.

Lesbos is prominent in Greek history and has many claims to literary distinction. It was the birthplace of Terpander, a famous musician of the 7th century B.C.; of Alcæus, a contemporary lyric poet; of Arion, a semi-mythical poet; and of Sappho, 7th century B.C. who wrote much poetry, some of which survives. She was praised by Plato and the Sapphic metre and stanza perpetuate her name. Many poets, from Ovid to Swinburne, have singled her out for praise or comment.

Lesbia was the name chosen by Catullus, the Roman poet and epigrammatist to salute the woman he loved; probably the notorious Clodia, wife of Metellus Celer.

The words lesbian, lesbianism (or Sapphism) derive from practices and perversions attributed to Sappho and her followers.

The isles of Greece, the isles of Greece!
Where burning Sappho loved and sung . . .
    Byron (1788–1824), *Don Juan.*

Horace says "still lives the heat imparted to the lyre by the Æolian fair (Sappho)."

Lethe of the Waters of Lethe, lethal, lethargic, etc. In Greek mythology Lethe (oblivion) was one of the rivers of Hades which the souls of the dead were required to taste in order to secure oblivion and the obliteration of all memories on reincarnation. Virgil describes the ghosts drinking at the river of Lethe before their reincarnation.

Alexander Pope (1688–1744), in *The Dunciad* (1728) refers to the Waters of Lethe, where old Bavius sits to dip poetic souls and blunt the sense.

Aristophanes refers to Lethe as a plain in Hades.

Lilliput of Lilliputian. The adjective Lilliputian, applied to any diminutive person or object, derives from Jonathan Swift's *Gulliver's Travels* (1726).

In this brilliant and fierce political satire, Lemuel Gulliver, "first a surgeon, and then a Captain of several ships," travels in Lilliput, the country of pigmies to whom Lemuel is a giant.

Swift (1667–1745) was born in Dublin, the posthumous son of well-connected parents. After a sojourn in Ireland as Canon of Kilroot, he resumed London activities and became immersed in politics and political propaganda. He ended his life, which was marred by brain disease, as Dean of St. Patrick's Cathedral, Dublin.

Limerick of the Limerick. The western county of Limerick in Eire gives its name to a popular form of five-line verse, generally nonsense verse, which is traditional. The rhyme is a a b b a, and the nursery rhyme, *Hickory, Dickory, Dock*, embodies the form.

Impromptu songs sung at Irish feasts for more than a century often devoted each verse to a different district or inhabitant thereof.

A refrain between each verse was said to start with the line *Will you come up to Limerick* or *We'll all come up, come up to Limerick.*

The name of the county and city was not applied to the verse form until much later. It was widely popularized by Edward Lear (1812–88) in his *Book of Nonsense* (1846) written for the grandchildren of his patron, the Earl of Derby.

The form became a literary fashion and attracted the pens of such writers as Rossetti, Swinburne and Ruskin.

A typical Lear Limerick is:

There was an Old Man with a beard,
Who said, "It is just as I feared!—
    Two Owls and a Hen,
    Four Larks and a Wren,
Have all built their nests in my beard!

Limoges of Limousine. The closed car or carriage, with a roof extending over the driver, derives its name of limousine from **Limoges**, the capital of the ancient French province of Limousin. The word was the feminine adjectival form for an inhabitant of the cathedral city or province. In the 12th century the province was in English control, as part of the dowry of Eleanor of Acquitaine.

The Hated Limousins were a group of cardinals from the province who, in the latter part of the 14th century, dominated the Papal Court, which was then at Avignon.

A celebrated family of French enamel painters and engravers in the 16th century, born at Limoges, took the name of Limousin, or Limosin.

Lincoln of Lincoln Green, College, Judgment, etc. The cathedral city and Midland county of Lincoln is noted for textiles, agricultural machinery and produce. In the days when counties made cloth of a characteristic colour, Lincoln was noted for a bright green cloth, as was Kendal, in Westmorland. Robin Hood and his men were habited in Kendal green.

Michael Drayton (1563–1631), in his *Poly-Olbion*, which sings the glories of England, refers to "Swains in shepherds' gray and girls in Lincoln green."

Lincoln College, Oxford, was founded in the 15th century by Richard Fleming, Bishop of Lincoln.

The Lincoln Judgment was a celebrated ecclesiastical suit in 1889 when the Bishop of Lincoln, Dr. Edward King, was cited before the Archbishop of Canterbury to answer charges of various ritual offences. Judgment given by the Archbishop confined itself to legal points and the Bishop was not admonished. The case is historic because of the questions of ritual that were decided and because of the legal confirmation of the right of the Archbishop to try a diocesan for ecclesiastical offences.

Lincoln's Inn, one of the four London Inns of Court, derives its name from the mansion of a 15th-century Earl of Lincoln built on the site which had previously belonged to the Black Friars.

The Lincoln Imp, famous throughout the world in the form of doorknockers, handles, "charms," etc., is a small carving in Lincoln Cathedral, which is also famous for its Angel Choir.

The Imp was copied and its possibilities developed last century by a noted Lincoln house of watchmakers and jewellers.

Lille of Lisle. The strong, twisted thread known as lisle is so called from the original name of the university city of Lille, in the north of France, south-east of Dunkirk and north of Arras. It is a leading manufacturing centre, producing large quantities of textiles with ancillary industries. Lille was occupied by the Germans during the First World War. The city houses the famous Pasteur Institute.

Llangollen of "The Ladies of Llangollen." The Welsh town of Llangollen, on the Dee, south-west of Wrexham, in Denbighshire, is a noted beauty spot. It is frequently cited in literature as the home of the eccentric "Ladies of Llangollen" or "The Ladies (or Maids) of the Vale."

The town to-day is a popular resort and supports textile, mining and allied industries.

The Vale was frequently named in Victorian picture-postcard days as the most beautiful scenic vista in Britain.

Its Ladies were Lady Eleanor Butler (?1745–1829) and Miss Sarah Ponsonby (?1745–1831). They lived in strange seclusion at a pseudo timbered house known as Plas Newydd—the New Place—on the hill just outside Llangollen. They never left the house for a night in fifty years.

The women, eccentric intellectuals in dress, manners and views, commanded the attention, correspondence and visits of the leading figures in literature, art, etc., of their day.

Remarkable company gathered there and strange rites were imposed upon the visitors. One demanded that at a second stay a guest should present to the house a carved oak panel commemorating his or her stay.

Wordsworth's visits resulted in his writing a sonnet on the Ladies, referring to Plas Newydd as "The Vale of Friendship," and to the Maids as *sisters in love, a love allowed to climb. Even on this earth, above the reach of Time!*

The Ladies took strong exception to the poet's reference therein to their "low-roofed Cot."

Lady Eleanor belonged to the Irish house of Ormonde; her brother succeeding to the Earldom in 1791. She and her companion are buried in the parish church at Llangollen, where there is also a monument erected by them to their maid.

The first Earl of Ormonde (1610–88) was the subject of an attempt upon his life by the Irish adventurer "Colonel" Thomas Blood, who almost succeeded on another occasion in stealing the Crown Jewels from the Tower of London.

Plas Newydd, with its many odd relics, has been preserved. It is now the headquarters of the Welsh National Theatre.

Lombard Street of "All Lombard Street to a China orange." Lombard Street, which runs from the Mansion House to Gracechurch Street, in the City of London, is a great banking centre. It takes its name from the former residence and activities in that neighbourhood of the Lombards, an Italian fraternity of bankers, merchants and money lenders who first came to England in the 13th century from Siena, Lucca and Florence. They were known collectively as The Lombards, though not all came from Lombardy.

They were banished by Queen Elizabeth but the street, often reputed to be the richest in the City, had already become a vast financial

centre. The saying "All Lombard Street to a China orange," which figures frequently in literature, implies the longest of odds; the prodigious wealth of London banking against a triviality.

Lombardy of the Lombardy Poplar. The northern Italian division of Lombardy gives its name to one of the most popular and instantly recognizable trees of Great Britain. The species, *P. pyramidalis*, or *P. italica*, was introduced from Lombardy in 1758, but probably originated in central Asia. The Poplars share with the willows a preference for damp places.

The rapid, vertical and plume-like growth of the Lombardy poplar makes it conspicuous in any company. The timber is of little value, though it is light and tough.

The poplars are of the aspen family, whose characteristic trembling or quivering leaf movement is referred to frequently in the Bible and other literature.

> *O woman! in our hours of ease,*
> *Uncertain, coy, and hard to please,*
> *And variable as the shade*
> *By the light quivering aspen made . . .*
> Scott, *Marmion* (1808).

The "twinkling" habit is due to the effect of the wind on the unusual leaf stem formation.

The White Poplar has an unexpectedly different leaf—similar in shape to that of the sycamore and plane—and a downy, white undersurface.

London of the London Plane, London Pride. The great metropolis has adopted and given its name to the tree which, above all others, accommodates itself to the City's grime and congestion and flourishes like the green bay tree in the most unlikely and seemingly uncongenial places.

The tree is the plane (*Platanus acerifolia*), generally known as the London plane.

The species, thought to be a hybrid between the Oriental and the Western Plane, has no known natural habitation and is thought to have appeared in the Oxford Botanic Garden in the 17th century.

Its leaf is similar to the sycamore, or False Plane, but without that leaf's red veining. It is characterized by pendant, rough ball-like greenish fruits (in contrast with the sycamore's red-brown, winged samaras). The plane's fruits are known to children as "knuckle-dusters" and their rough surface, together with their sturdy attachment, makes them a mildly painful juvenile weapon.

The trunk of the London plane is immediately recognizable by its dappled appearance. This is caused by the patchy, irregular shedding of the outer bark, due to the expansion of the lower layers. The bark is in fact naturally light grey, but London grime and fog turns it to the familiar black.

The tree thrives when planted in streets and can be found, offering attractive appearance and dense shade, in the most unlikely and congested spots. It will flourish in dark corners, between houses, and will suffer paving stones, asphalt or even concrete to encroach over its roots to the trunk itself.

London Pride, one of the best known mountain saxifrages, earns its name for a similar sturdy resistance to the City's horticultural handicaps. It is found also in southern Ireland and is known variously as St. Patrick's cabbage and None-so-Pretty. Its perky coral-pink spikes of blossom rise from a circle of leathery leaves. It survives smoke, fog and lack of good soil, and flourishes on neglect.

Lord's of Lord's. The name Lord's is universally recognized as synonymous with cricket and places the ground which is the Mecca of the game. The ground, at St. John's Wood, London, N.W., has been the headquarters of the M.C.C. (Maryle-bone Cricket Club) since its inception in 1787. It is also the home ground of the Middlesex County Cricket team. It owes its name to a Yorkshire man, Thomas Lord, who first rented a ground in Dorset Square, then a rural area, and at each subsequent move took with him the famous original turf.

Lorelei of the Lorelei. The Lorelei, a seductive siren frequently mentioned in literature, takes her name from the Lorelei Rock which rises out of the Rhine, near St. Goar, in Prussia.

The maiden was said to sit upon the rock, singing sweetly while combing her glorious hair. Thus she lured passing sailors too near the rock and to their death. The rock, which possesses a noted echo, is also cited as the hiding-place of the treasure of the Nibelungen, the subject of the famous Wagner Ring cycle, composed 1853–70, produced 1869–76.

The Lorelei, sometimes spelt Lurlei, is the subject of a poem by Heine (1797–1856).

Lucca of Lucca Oil. The fine quality of olive oil known as Lucca was originally primarily produced in the province of that name in Tuscany. It is east of Florence and its capital, of the same name, is an ancient cathedral city annexed to Italy in the 19th century. It has many Roman remains.

The chief manufacturing industries are fine textiles.

Lyceum of Lyceum. The grove and gymnasium outside Athens, known as the Lyceum, was sacred to Apollo Lyceus. Here the followers of Aristotle gathered to be taught his philosophy.

The name is still in frequent use for theatres, academies and similar educational institutions.

The famous Lyceum Theatre in London, closely associated with Sir

Henry Irving (1838–1905), was originally built in 1794 and known as the English Opera House. It was rebuilt, after destruction by fire, in 1834.

Lydd of **Liddite.** The high explosive known as Lyddite, of which picric acid is a chief component, is named from the Kentish borough of Lydd, near the Cinque Port of Romney. It was upon the government artillery ranges there that the explosive was first tested in about 1888.

Mangkasara of Macassar, anti-macassar. The Dutch East Indies port of Mangkasara, or Macassar, is situated on the west coast of the island of Celebes. The Strait of Macassar separates Celebes from Borneo. The port has a large trade in coffee, copra, spices and trepang, the edible sea slug.

The local Macassar oil was much favoured as a hair-dressing and as an ingredient in pomades, etc., during the Victorian and Edwardian eras. In consequence the coverings thrown over the back of chairs, etc., to prevent grease marks, and sometimes merely as an ornament, were known as antimacassars.

In virtues nothing earthly could surpass her,
Save thine "incomparable oil," Macassar!
        Byron, *Don Juan* (1819).

Macouba of Maccaboy or Maccabaw. The distinctive snuff, usually scented with attar of roses and known as maccaboy, or maccabaw, is named from the Macouba district in French Martinique, in the Windward Islands, north of the British Trinidad and Tobago. The volcano, Mont Pelle, is the highest point of the island and its eruption in 1902 destroyed the town of St. Pierre and resulted in 25,000 casualties. There is a large trade in sugar, coffee, etc.

The island, which was discovered by the Spanish in the 15th century, was in British hands during the 18th century and was ceded to France in 1814. It is a French naval station.

Snuff-taking became common in England in the 17th century and it was at first the custom freshly to grate it (*râper*) for each use. A coarse type of snuff is still known as rappee.

Madeira of Madeira wine and cake. Madeira is the chief island of a volcanic archipelago some 400 miles east of Morocco and north of Canary Islands. The island was discovered in the 15th century and settled by the Portuguese, to whom it still belongs. In addition to the vineyards, now less extensive, there are sugar plantations and a tourist trade. Madeira wine, generally not dissimilar from sherry, is made from black and white grapes. The vines were originally brought from Cyprus or Crete and flourished in the mellow climate.

Maelström of Maelström. Though the term maelström is now applied to any considerable whirlpool, or even to a swirling mass of people, it is in fact the name of a specific and dangerous whirlpool which appears occasionally near the island of Moskoe, off the north-west coast of Norway, in the Lofoten islands. In certain tides and winds it can be fatal to small craft.

Edgar Allan Poe (1809–49) wrote an imaginary description *A Descent into the Maelström* (1841). The whirlpool was traditionally thought to be the entrance to a subterranean chasm or tunnel.

Mafeking of to maffick, mafficking. To exult riotously, or to celebrate a national or lesser event with extravagant scenes is known as "To maffick," from the original celebrations in London of the Relief of Mafeking on May 18, 1900.

The town of Mafeking, in British Bechuanaland, South Africa, in the gold mining area, was subjected to a long and bitter siege during the Boer War. It was defended with brilliant ingenuity and endurance for six months by Colonel Robert Baden-Powell, afterwards Lord Baden-Powell of Gilwell (1857–1941), founder of the Boy Scout Movement and Chief Scout of the World. It was relieved by Colonel Plumer, afterwards Field Marshal Lord Plumer. The news of its relief was the occasion in London for widespread public demonstration and rejoicing.

Magdala of Magdalene, maudlin. The Galilean town of Magdala on the west coast of Lake Gennesaret (*Matt. xv. 39*) gave its name specifically in the form Magdalene to the inhabitants thereof. Its wider significance, to denote a reformed prostitute, derives from Mary Magdalene, or of Magdala. She is first mentioned in the Bible as having had seven devils cast out of her (*Luke viii. 2*) and as ministering to Christ of her substance. She watches at the Cross, attends Christ's burial and anoints the body. She is the first to see the risen Saviour. She supposes Him to be the gardener, but He speaks to her by name (*John xx. 11–18*). Authorities are divided as to whether the woman in *Luke vii* with the alabaster box of ointment should be identified as Mary Magdalene.

The word "maudlin," to denote mawkish sentimentality or a tearful state of intoxication, derives from the same source, probably in particular reference to the frequent portrayal in early art of Mary Magdalene as a weeping figure. Asylums for women fallen from chastity were for many years known as Magdalene Asylums, or merely Magdalenes.

Magdalen College and Bridge are among the most famous sights of Oxford.

Magenta of Magenta. Magenta is a town in Lombardy, Italy, some 15 miles west of Milan. It is famous for the battle in 1859 when the allied French and Sardinians defeated the Austrians.

The brilliant crimson aniline dye was discovered soon after the battle, from which it took its name. Magenta, rubine, roseine and other names are applied industrially to the dyestuff fuchsine and its colour, which is similar to that of the fuchsia flower, named after Leonhard Fuchs (1501–66), the noted German botanist. The dye is also used for colouring confectionery, wines, etc.

Hungary of Magyar. The Magyars, who for centuries have been a dominant race in Hungary, came originally from the Carpathian plains.

A distinctive feature of their national dress gives rise to the term Magyar, from the Magyar blouse, indicating a garment with sleeves cut in one piece with the article.

Majorca of Majolica. Majolica, which term now covers many imitations, is properly applied to Italian ware, the characteristic of which is an enamel with a fired painted decoration.

The ware is thought to have been first made in Majorca, the largest of the Balearic Islands, in the Mediterranean, off the east coast of Spain. The term may have been applied generally to Spanish lustre ware imported into Italy from the Balearic Islands generally. (See *Faenza of Faience*.)

Malacca of Malacca. The rich brown Malacca canes, chiefly seen as walking-sticks, are grown in the district of Malacca on the west coast of the Malay Peninsula. The Strait of Malacca—the name derives from *melaka*, a local jungle fruit—separates the Malay peninsula from Sumatra. The cane is obtained from the stem of a local palm.

Malaga of Malaga. The noted white wine, Malaga, largely produced from muscatel grapes, is named from its chief source, the Spanish seaport of Malaga, on the Mediterranean, north-east of Gibraltar. It is a cathedral city with a large trade in wine, olives, fruit, etc., and also cigars, sugar and metals.

Château Malmaison of Malmaison. The type of carnation known as the malmaison was grown profusely in the Château Malmaison a few miles west of Paris, in the department of the Seine, which was the residence of the Empress Joséphine after her divorce from Napoleon. There she died.

Maria Rose Joséphine (1763–1814) was Napoleon's first wife. She had a profound influence over the Emperor and was the focus of a brilliant court. The marriage was unfruitful and was dissolved in 1809.

Malta, G.C. of the Maltese Cross, etc. Malta, the Mediterranean island stronghold which was awarded the George Cross for superb survival of its siege during the Second World War, is primarily associated in the public mind with the characteristic Maltese Cross. The Cross, shaped thus ✠, was originally the badge of the Knights Hospitallers, a religious brotherhood of St. John at Jerusalem founded during the 11th century to care for the visitors to the Holy Sepulchre. They included a strong military force. In the 14th century they occupied the island of Rhodes and in the 15th century, their power diminished, they found shelter in Malta and took a large part of the island's administration.

The distinctive mark of the Order was the wearing on the black habit of a cross formed by the meeting of four barbed arrow heads.

The characteristic cross has been embodied in many orders and medals, notably the Victoria Cross and the German Iron Cross. In modified form it appears in the badge of the Order of Merit and elsewhere. Originally it was the badge of the Red Cross, established under the Geneva Convention, 1864, but now the Greek Cross is used, in red on white—the reversal of the Swiss flag.

The Maltese dog, incorrectly called a Maltese Terrier, is an ancient breed of lap dog; white with long silky hair.

The breed can be traced for 2,000 years, but authorities are not certain that it originated in the island. It has similarity with lap dogs of other parts of Europe, many of which, as in the case of the Maltese, were bred small enough to be carried in the sleeves of owners at the Imperial Courts of Rome.

The breed was popularized in Britain about 1860.

There is a local type of cat known as the Maltese and the name is also to be found in Malta, or Mediterranean, Fever, attributed to infected milk from Maltese goats.

Manchester of the Manchester Terrier. The Black and Tan terrier was never particularly associated with Manchester save in the support that Mr. S. Handley of Manchester gave to the breed in the 1870s. He was largely responsible for its acceptance and popularity and the name Manchester Terrier was given to record and honour his work.

The terriers, not now as widely popular, are good house dogs and efficient ratters.

Manhattan and Bronx of the Cocktails. Manhattan, one of the five boroughs of New York City, is an island between the Hudson and the East rivers. Through it runs Broadway, the longest street in the world, and the greatest business centre. Its 16 miles from the southern tip of the island pass through great civic, commercial and amusement centres. Broadway itself has given its name to the peak of show business. A Broadway success is the ultimate seal of commercial success; to be "on Broadway" is every dramatist's and actor's ambition.

The Bronx is another and northernmost borough of New York City. It was constituted in 1898. It was formerly a district in Westchester county, New York. Harlem, which contains the famous coloured quarter, is one of its boundaries.

Manila of Manila hemp, cheroot, etc. The capital and chief port of the Philippines, East Indies, Manila (or Manilla), gives its name to the local grown *Musa textilis*, whose coarser fibres are used for ropes, matting, sailcloth, etc. The finer textures of the Manila hemp are made into handkerchiefs, scarves and similar material. Some are used in coarse but durable paper.

Manila, one of the greatest hemp ports in the world, is on the west coast of the island of Luzon. Sugar, oils, tobacco, etc., are also exported. There is a local cheroot known as a Manila.

The manilla, a metal bangle used by certain African tribes as currency, does not derive its name from the Philippine capital but from the Latin *manus*, a hand.

The Mansion House of Mansion House. The term Mansion House in London implies the domain and jurisdiction of the Lord Mayor, much in the same way as Downing Street (*q.v.*) is synonymous with the Prime Minister's office and pronouncements, and the Kremlin (*q.v.*) with the Soviet's policy.

The Mansion House is at the end of Cheapside, near the Royal Exchange and the Bank of England. It is the official residence of the Lord Mayor, who is Chief Citizen of London and whose permission even the King is required to seek, in formal ceremony at the City gate, before he can enter the City.

The present building was erected in 1750 and has been the scene of many historic, diplomatic and social ceremonies. Prior to its erection Lord Mayors held office in their own homes or temporarily occupied suitable City premises during the Mayoralty.

A substantial contribution to the cost of the erection of the Mansion House was made by fines of citizens who refused for various reasons to serve as sheriffs.

The first Lord Mayor to occupy the Mansion House was Sir Crisp Gasgoigne, in 1753. It houses the priceless City plate and regalia. The dining-room is the famous Egyptian Hall and the Justice Room is one of the City Police Courts.

Isle of Man of Manx, Manx cat, etc. Authorities differ on the origin of the word Manx as applied to the Isle of Man. Most trace it from the Old Norse *manskr*, of Man, and the name of the island from Mannin (middle) as the island is situated in the Irish Sea almost equidistant between Ireland and England.

The island is a popular holiday resort, encouraged by an equable climate and semi-tropical vegetation. There is much mining in the island; metals, including silver, but no coal. Granite, marble and greenstone are quarried.

The Celtic inhabitants had Welsh kings, followed by a Scandinavian dynasty after the 9th century. In the 13th century the rights were ceded to Scotland. The island was later granted to the Earls of Derby before purchase by the British Government from the Duke of Atholl in 1829.

The Isle of Man has its own Government, council and legislative assembly, known as the House of Keys, or *Tynwald*. The origin of the word Keys is generally thought to be the implication that the keys unlocked the law.

The capital is Douglas and the island forms the diocese of the Bishop of Sodor and Man. The "Sodor" is an historic and little known survival from the days of the Vikings. In the 9th century Harold, King of Norway, developed the Viking conquests of Norway and Shetland, which he named the Kingdom of the Northern Isles, or the Nordreys. The Western Isles he named the Sudreys, or Southern Isles, and the Isle of Man, after its conquest, became associated with them politically and ecclesiastically. Up to the 13th century, when control of the islands passed to Scotland, the

Sudreys and Man were a constitutional unit and the latter had the predominating representation.

Morocco of Marocain, Morocco leather. The dress fabric, marocain, made in silk and allied materials, takes its name from the French for Moroccan. It was originally made in the north-west African country.

Morocco leather, originating in Morocco but now also made in Europe, was first the product of goats' skins tanned with sumac, the leaves of which tree or shrub are ground and used extensively in dyeing and tanning. French morocco is a smaller grained, similar type of leather and Levant morocco a large grained, superior product.

Marsala of Marsala. The fortified seaport and cathedral city of Marsala, on the western extremity of Sicily, is in the province of Trapani. It gives its name to the local dry, sweet wine, resembling sherry, and also to other wines of Sicily which are fortified there. The district supports an extensive trade in grain, oil and brandy, and there are noted salt mines and marble caves. It is the site of Garibaldi's landing in 1860.

The introduction of Marsala into Britain is said to have been due to naval officers of the Mediterranean Squadron during the Napoleonic wars. They favoured it when Port wine was unobtainable.

Other Sicilian wines whose names derive from places include Etna and Moscato di Pontelleria; the latter from the volcanic island south-west of Sicily.

Marseilles of The Marseillaise. Marseilles, the great French and Mediterranean seaport, is situated on the Gulf of Lyon. Its fortifications include the adjacent islands of If. The name If derives from the fact that they were once covered with yews. The Chateau D'If, once a State Prison, crowns the island and

is made famous in literature through Dumas' *Count of Monte Cristo* (1854-5).

Marseilles was founded by a Greek colony about 600 B.C.

The Marseillaise, the French National Anthem, was written and composed by Claude Rouget de Lisle (1760–1835) in 1792. He was a captain in a corps of engineers and is said to have written and composed the song in a day. The Mayor of Strasbourg, where de Lisle was stationed, called for a patriotic song to rouse the men to the defence of Strasbourg when war was declared against Austria.

The song's first title was *Chant de l'Armée du Rhin*. Its reception was sensational and when, in July, 1792, the volunteers from Marseilles sang it as they entered Paris, and at the storming of the Tuileries a month later, the song spread like a flame and acquired its present name. The Song of the Revolution was forbidden by Napoleon and the Bourbons, but it rose again, imperishable.

Mortella of Martello tower. The pill-box type of coast and river-bank fortification, known as the Martello Tower, was named corruptly from Cape Mortella, in Corsica.

When, in 1794, a British Fleet under Lord Hood supported the Corsican insurgents, their attack was held up by a strong round tower. The authorities were so impressed by the resistance of this type of fortification that many Martello towers were built in the following years round the English coasts to repel the threatened Napoleonic invasions. The towers, some of which remain, were about 40 ft. in height.

Tomb of Mausolus of Mausoleum. The tomb of Mausolus, king of Caria, was erected at Halicarnassus by his widow, Artemisia, in 353 B.C. It was accounted one of the Seven Wonders of the World.

The ornate sepulchre, over 100 ft. high and surmounted by a group of statuary which included figures of Mausolus and his wife, gave rise to the word mausoleum. The word is still widely applied to any ornate tomb of considerable dimensions.

The original survived in good condition until the 12th century, and remains of the monument were brought to England in the 19th century and placed in the British Museum.

Mayfair of Mayfair. The word Mayfair, from the district of the west end of London, is used as a synonym for stylish, sophisticated society and life. The district lies within the square of Park Lane, Oxford Street, Regent Street and Piccadilly. It includes many of London's most exclusive hotels and fashionable residences.

The area is so named from a fair that was formerly held there each May.

Mazovia of Mazurka. Mazovia, a former independent district in the north of Russian Poland, gave its name to the gay Polish dance, similar to the polka, and to the music thereof. It is generally written in three-eight or three-four time and the form was much favoured by the Polish composer, Chopin. The word mazurka is Polish for a woman of Mazovia.

Meander of "to meander." The river Mæander, or Maiandros, in Phrygia, was noted among the Greeks for its sinuous, winding course. The appellative use of the name gives our word, meander, which, while correctly applied to the circuitous path of a river, is also used to describe any circuitous journey or a wandering at random.

The derivative word, meandrine, means full of windings or convolutions.

Mecca of Mecca. Mecca is the capital of Hedjaz, the Arabian province flanked on the west by the Red Sea. It is an ancient city and the birthplace of Mohammed (or, more properly, Muhammad). It is therefore the most holy city of Islam and the focus of the faith.

The word Mecca is now in general usage to denote the focal point of any widely known interest or organization: "Lord's is the Mecca of cricket; Wimbledon the Mecca of tennis."

The city is a place of incessant pilgrimage, and its floating population largely subsists in catering for the pilgrims and in maintaining the mosques and other buildings. The chief Mosque holds over 30,000 people. It contains the Kaâba, a shrine said to have been built by Abraham on the site of Adam's expulsion from Paradise. The Kaâba had been the sanctuary of Mecca long before Mohammed's age and built into one of its walls was the famous "black stone," held by tradition to have been brought from Paradise by the archangel Gabriel. For over 1,300 years it has been a precious relic, worn smooth by the kisses of the faithful. During the siege of the city, after Mohammed's death, it was fractured by fire. It was once captured by Carmathian marauders and was retrieved by ransom after over twenty years.

The stone is only a few inches square and is thought by some authorities to be a meteorite.

Malines of Mechlin lace, the Malines Conversations. The Belgian cathedral city of Malines, a few miles south-east of Antwerp, is also known as Mechlin and that name was given to its formerly famous lace manufactures. Textiles and tapestries now take more prominence in the city's trade.

Cardinal Mercier, Archbishop of Malines and Primate of Belgium, was one of the great figures of the First World War.

The Malines Conversations, due to the Archbishop's writings, were an historic meeting between Roman

Catholic and Anglican ecclesiastics in 1923–4.

Melton Mowbray of Melton, Melton Mowbray pies. The Leicestershire market town of Melton Mowbray, north-east of the county town, produces a local cloth for men, known as Melton. The town is in hunting country and has always claimed good tailoring. Melton Mowbray is also famed for local made pork pies and for Stilton cheese. There is a considerable iron industry on the outskirts of the town.

Men's "pork pie" hats were frequently referred to as "Meltons."

Milan of Milliner. The province and city of Milan, in Northern Italy, was once arbiter of elegance and dress fashion; a position since largely usurped by Paris, London and New York.

The word milliner derives from a Milan merchant, or Milaner; a vendor of Milan wares.

Originally the word was essentially masculine in its implication, and the term "milliner's wife" was used for the women who first entered the trade. The word milliner then gradually assumed a derogatory meaning, applicable to fussy and effeminate men. Thus Hotspur, in *Henry IV*:

> *He was perfuméd like a milliner;*
> *And 'twixt his finger and his thumb he held*
> *A pouncet-box, which ever and anon*
> *He gave his nose, and took't away again.*

A pouncet-box was a perforated container for perfume. It was often made in metal, in elaborate design, and sometimes fitted with lock and key. There was generally a handle for carrying like a handbag.

To-day the term milliner is primarily feminine in its application and reserved for those concerned with the creation and marketing of women's hats and other feminine head coverings.

Mincing Lane of Mincing Lane. The London thoroughfare of Mincing Lane, running from Fenchurch Street to Great Tower Street, between and north of London and Tower Bridges, is the centre of the wholesale tea, sugar and allied trades. The term is widely used as a synonym for such activities.

The lane has been so-named for centuries, with modifications of spelling, and its origin is thought to have been from an Anglo-Saxon word *mynechenn*, meaning a nun. Religious orders in former years occupied premises there.

Queen Elizabeth granted a charter for the erection of the adjoining wharves in the 16th century.

Minorca of Minorca fowl. The black variety of fowl known as the Minorca was originally brought from Spain and takes its name from the Spanish Balearic Islands in the Mediterranean. Minorca is the second largest of the group and supports agriculture and fruit-growing, cattle- and horse-breeding.

Mizpah of Mizpah ring. The Mizpah ring, popular in earlier times as a love-token, was a ring inscribed with the name in reference to *Gen. xxxi. 48–9*: "Therefore was the name of it . . . Mizpah, for he said, The Lord watch between me and thee, when we are absent one from another."

Mizpah (meaning "watch-tower") was the place in Gilead where Laban and Jacob set up a heap of stones as a memorial of their parting and as a covenant between them.

Mocha of Mocha coffee. The fortified seaport of Mocha, or Mokha, was the former capital of Yemen, Arabia, on the Red Sea. It is near Aden. Its former famous trade in coffee has now been to some extent diverted through Hodeida, a port some 100 miles north, on the Red Sea.

A mocha is also a species of chalcedony, a semi-precious stone in the quartz category. Mochas are characterized by brown or black moss-like patterns and to-day are mined primarily in India.

Moravia of the Moravian Church. Formerly margravate and crownland of Austria, the province of Moravia, in Czechoslovakia, sustains its name in the Moravian Church, or the Bohemian Brethren.

They are a Protestant sect, claiming origins in the 15th century. The sect was constituted at Prague and at one time claimed many hundreds of churches and centres of communion. The church, which now has four provinces, German, British, North American and South American, has been characterized by its strong missionary zeal. It has cordial relationship with Nonconformists and, when the project was mooted at the beginning of this century that the Moravians should enter into closer relationship with the Church of England, the sect intimated its sympathy in principle but preferred to maintain its distinct entity.

There are some forty congregations and preaching centres at present in the British Isles, with a membership of over 3,000.

Moselle of Moselle. The river Moselle, that gives its name to the wine made from the vineyards on its banks, is a tributary of the Rhine. It rises in France in the department of the Vosges and joins the Rhine at Coblenz. Most of the wine, which is white, comes from the German territory. It is usually marketed in blue-green bottles.

Mosul of Muslin. Mosul, the capital of Iraq, is on the river Tigris, almost due north of Bagdad. It was formerly famous for a large cotton industry which gave the name muslin to its particular products.

Muslin resembles gauze (*q.v.*), but is woven without twisting the crossing threads. Many muslins of supremely fine texture are made in India, and the material is also manufactured extensively in Europe.

Nanking of Nankeen. The cotton cloth known as nankeen was originally manufactured in Nanking, the ancient capital of China. Trousers made of this material were known as nankeens. The local grown cotton was a natural characteristic yellow so that the word was, and is, applied to that colour, irrespective of the material presenting it.

Naples of "See Naples and die," Neapolitan. Although John Fletcher (1579–1625) called Naples "the Paradise of Italy," there would appear to be no historical reason why this of all the world's noble cities should be singled out for the saying "See Naples and die." It has, however, a fair claim to the distinction of the proverb which appears in several languages, including Italian.

The Neapolitan ice is a product of Naples that has found favour elsewhere. Its characteristic is the formation in layers, each of a different colour and flavour. The name Neapolitan is given also to pastries and similar confections made on the same principle.

The Neapolitan violet is a double, sweet scented variety.

The Neapolitan Mud Flower is a species of yellow sea anemone

Nazareth of "Can there any good thing come out of Nazareth?" The question is asked by Nathanael, in *John i. 46*, when Philip claims that they have found Him of whom Moses and the prophets wrote, Jesus of Nazareth. The implication, that nothing significant is likely to come out of an insignificant place, is still conveyed in this phrase to-day.

Though Christ was born in Bethlehem, He was brought up in Nazareth, the town of Lower Galilee, the place of the Annunciation. It had been a place despised.

Newcastle-on-Tyne of Newcastle disease, etc. The virulent infectious poultry disease, which often assumes epidemic proportions and causes severe losses, is named after Newcastle-upon-Tyne because it was first reported there on a serious scale in the 1920s. It has affected the poultry industry in several countries and little is known of its origin or of its certain prevention or cure.

The expression "to send (or carry) coals to Newcastle" is a tribute to the great coaling port and implies a superfluity or the sending of something to a place where it is already abundant.

Newfoundland of the Newfoundland dog. The great British island of Newfoundland, on the Gulf of St. Lawrence, has an area of over 40,000 square miles. It supports fishing and timber industries and has extensive modern paper mills responsible for a large proportion of British imports of paper.

The Newfoundland dog, noted for its devotion and sagacity, is frequently mentioned in literature and the breed was the subject of a famous picture by Landseer entitled "A Distinguished Member of the Humane Society."

The breed has been known for centuries and widely exported. The dogs were used for haulage, as guards and as retrievers. They survive severe conditions and have been trained for life-saving and for Arctic exploration.

The Newfoundland, which to the layman looks like a cross between a St. Bernard and a long-coated retriever, is preferred nowadays in black or black and white. Earlier colours of red are not now favoured.

The thick oily coat and partly

webbed feet make the Newfoundland an excellent water dog. In Britain the Newfoundland Club was formed in 1884.

Burns mentions the breed and Byron, in his *Epitaph* on his Newfoundland, ascribes to the breed "Beauty without vanity, strength without insolence, courage without ferocity, and all the virtues of man without his vices."

Newgate of *The Newgate Calender,* **Newgate fashion, etc.** Newgate, one of the gates in the wall of ancient London, first became prominent in its association with crime when the rooms over the gate itself were used as cells. Then the first of several great prisons was built on the site in the 15th century, and Newgate became the name applied popularly to any gaols. Newgate was the City of Middlesex gaol for centuries and *The Newgate Calendar*, a biographical record of some of the most infamous criminals confined there, became a classic dossier of contemporary crime and a document much quoted and drawn upon in history and historical fiction. It first appeared in the 18th century and there were many subsequent editions.

Famous names are associated with Newgate. In the 15th century Sir Richard (Dick) Whittington left funds for its rebuilding, it was destroyed in the Great Fire, 1666, and was severely damaged in the No Popery Riots of 1780 when many prisoners escaped.

It was the scene of Mrs. Elizabeth Fry's labours in prison reform at the opening of the 19th century. Its many notable prisoners included William Penn, the Quaker founder of Pennsylvania, Titus Oates and Daniel Defoe.

Newgate at the time of the Anti-Popery Riots figures prominently in Dickens' *Barnaby Rudge* (1841).

Newgate fashion, which Shakespeare mentions in *1 Henry IV, iii. 3*, meant two-by-two, the mode by which prisoners were conveyed manacled together, to Newgate prison.

Two phrases embodying the name have now died out. They were "Newgate fringe," applying to hair between the chin and the larynx (an allusion to the position of the hangman's rope), and "Newgate knocker." The latter was a lock of hair favoured by costermongers and others. It was thought to resemble a knocker and many of the wearers had been or were potential inmates of the prison. It can be seen in contemporary art.

Newgate Street, east of St. Paul's, still exists and is the site of the Central Criminal Court, or Old Bailey (*q.v.*).

Newmarket of Newmarket. The market town of Newmarket, famous for its horse races, is 13 miles east-north-east of Cambridge, in the counties of Cambridgeshire and Suffolk.

There is extensive malting and brewing in the district, but it is racing that gives the town fame. Its course is one of the finest in the world and the Jockey Club is a noted institution.

At Newmarket are run many famous races, including the Two Thousand Guineas (1 mile; instituted 1809); the One Thousand Guineas (1 mile; 1814); The Jockey Club Stakes (1 mile 6 furlongs; 1801); the Autumn Double—The Cambridgeshire (1 mile 1 furlong; 1839); and the Cesarewitch (2 miles 2 furlongs 35 yards ; 1839).

The Guineas races are two of the five Classics, the others being the Derby (1780), the Oaks (1779) and the St. Leger (1776).

A Newmarket coat, or Newmarket, was a close-fitting overcoat for either sex, designed and supported by the racing population. The town's name is also found in the card game which originated in Newmarket and is now played all over the world, though its popularity has diminished.

Niagara of Niagara Falls. The term Niagara may be used broadly to describe any great cataract, torrent or even a clamour of words or noise. "To shoot Niagara" means to incur fearful risks.

Such uses of the word derive from the outstanding magnificence and terror of the Niagara Falls, on the lower Niagara river which connects Lake Erie with Lake Ontario. For volume of water the falls are the greatest in the world. The American Fall is over 1,000 ft. wide, with a sheer drop of 167 ft. and the adjacent Horse Shoe Fall, on the Canadian side, has a depth of over 150 ft.

The overall curve of rock measures more than a thousand yards and the mass of the Fall is estimated to be over 20 ft. in thickness.

Great parks flank the Falls which terminate in a seething whirlpool before the river enters Lake Ontario.

Charles Blondin (1824–97), the famous tight-rope walker, crossed the Falls many times on a rope suspended 160 ft. above them. His first successful accomplishment of the feat was followed by variations, including a blindfold performance, wheeling a barrow across and crossing the rope on stilts.

Nicæa of the Nicene Creed. Nicæa, the city of ancient Bithynia, in Asia Minor, bounded on the north by the Black Sea, was the site of two historic Œcumenical Councils; the first in 325 and the seventh in 787. At the former the Nicene Creed, the only creed to receive œcumenical sanction, was drawn up. It concluded with the clause "And I believe in the Holy Ghost."

The creed was confirmed by the Council of Constantinople in 381, when the additional clauses as they stand to-day were added, with the exception of one clause, the *filioque*, which pronounces that "the Holy Ghost proceedeth from the Father and the Son." This clause was added in the fifth or sixth century.

The two other creeds of the Church are the Apostles' and the Athanasian.

Nod of the Land of Nod. The expression "to go to the land of Nod" —to go to sleep—with parallel allusions in other languages, derives in name, with the felicity of association, from the Biblical district to which Cain fled (*Gen. iv. 16*). The name means "wandering," and the district appears to have been east of Eden, but may have been the general description applied to any land of wandering and wanderers.

Norfolk of Norfolk jacket, dumpling, Norfolk-Howards, etc. The east England maritime county of Norfolk has given its name to a man's loose jacket, now less widely seen, the chief characteristic of which is the waistband, generally but not always detachable.

Norfolk dumplings, originating in the county but widely popular, are made of dough with salt and boiling water. They should be about the size of a small egg and can be served in soups, etc., or as a sweet with jam, syrup, etc. "Norfolk dumpling" is also a term applied to inhabitants of the county in the same way, and as unfairly, as the neighbouring county is called "Silly Suffolk."

Norfolk-Howards is a slang term for bed-bugs. The origin is confused. Dr. Brewer associated it with the great names of Norfolk, that of its Duke (who is the premier Earl and the Hereditary Earl Marshal of England, and whose family name is Howard) and a possibly spurious advertisement which certainly appeared in *The Times* in 1862.

In it one James Bug, a native of Epsom and licensee of the Swan Tavern in Wakefield, renounces his surname and claims to adopt legally the name of Norfolk Howard.

The county name also appears in Norfolk capon, which is a red herring; in the Norfolk plover, which is the stone curlew, and in specifying the county's famous breed of turkeys.

Norwich of the Norwich Terrier, Norwich canary. The East Anglian cathedral city gives its name to a locally bred breed of terrier which, while known for some sixty years, has been officially recognized only since the formation of the Norwich Terrier Club in 1932. It was recognized several years later in the United States where it is generally known as the Jones Terrier. The breed is rough haired, with a docked tail and generally red in variations.

The term Norwich canary is a tribute to the city's pre-eminence in the British Isles as a centre for the breeding and exhibition of canaries and allied cage birds. (See *Canary*.)

Oberammergau of the Oberammergau Passion Play. The Upper Bavarian village of Oberammergau, south-west of Munich, is primarily occupied in peasant crafts, including wood and stone carving. It is world-famous for its Passion Play, in which the parts are taken by local inhabitants, often qualified by the natural succession of inheritance. It is performed every ten years in fulfilment of a vow made in the 17th century when the village was scourged by a severe plague. The original text has been several times revised. The performance draws visitors from all over the world.

Old Bailey of Old Bailey. Old Bailey, frequently but incorrectly referred to as The Old Bailey, is a street in London, in the parish of Smithfield. The term is used by the public to refer to the Central Criminal Courts which are at the north end. Here many notable trials are held. The name is thought to be a corruption of Balehill, the hill on which stood the Bale, or bailiff's house. It is believed to have been the scene of a court for many centuries. The present Court buildings, erected at the beginning of this century, occupy much of the site of the old Newgate Prison.

The Old Vic. The Old Vic., one of the few noted London theatres south of the Thames, was opened in 1818, soon after Waterloo, and is adjacent to the Waterloo terminus. It was renamed in honour of the young Princess Victoria.

Keen and Paganini appeared at the Old Vic., but its present fame began when Emma Cons (1837–1912), rescued it from melodrama and laid the foundations of its world acceptance as a centre of Shakespearian and other classical and modern productions at popular prices, and for the training of notable companies.

Emma Cons, founder of the Old Vic., was an alderman of the London County Council, a lover of beauty and a pupil of Ruskin. She secured royal support for her work, which was ably carried on by her niece Lilian Baylis, C.H. (d. 1937). Lilian Baylis was a woman of immense drive, personality and devotion to her profession. Her constant prayer was for good actors and actresses—cheap. She lived to see the Old Vic. become synonymous with notable—particularly Shakespearian—productions for the masses. Great names in the theatre gladly assisted her and she made many stars. The Old Vic. company, with its implicit standards and evangelistic zeal, has toured extensively and become famous throughout the world.

The theatre, which was closed by bomb damage in 1940, reopened on November 14, 1950.

Olympia of Olympia. The sacred plain of Olympia was in Elis, Peloponnese, the southern part of Greece, joined by the Isthmus of Corinth. It contained the Olympium, or temple of Zeus Olympius. It also contained the Stadium and the Hippodrome. Olympia was the second religious centre of the Greeks and was the scene of the Olympian Games, the epic contests held every four years. Records were kept of the winners from 776 B.C. and the games, which were at first of local interest, eventually attracted entries from all over the Peloponnese. There were supporting fairs and the vast concourse attending—the Stadium held 40,000 people—attracted poets and orators.

The term Olympiad, now often incorrectly used to describe the modern Olympic Games, denotes in fact the four year period between the meetings, the period maintained to-day.

The name Hippodrome, still equally familiar for places of public amusement, derived from *hippos*, a horse, and was originally applied to the scene of chariot races, circuses, etc.

Orange of William of Orange, Orangemen. The French town of Orange is on the Rhone, just north of Avignon, the former Papal seat, and north-north-west of Marseilles. It was the capital of an independent principality for 500 years until the 16th century. In 1531 it passed to the House of Nassau, one of whose distinguished members, William of Orange, became William the Third of England (1650–1702). He was the posthumous son of William II, Prince of Orange, and Mary, daughter of Charles the First.

The name continues in the title of the ruler of the Netherlands, which runs: "By the Grace of God, Queen of the Netherlands, Princess of Orange-Nassau, etc."

Orange Lodges and Orangemen are terms applied to Irish Protestant organizations and their members. The Orange society, which was secret, was founded in 1795. It was named after William of Orange and kept as its festivals the anniversaries of the Battle of the Boyne and the Battle of Aughrim, or Aghrim, Co. Galway, scenes of two victories of William. The Orangemen, whose avowed intention was to secure Protestant ascendancy wherever possible, and whose Lodges extended to many countries, frequently prejudiced their cause by violence and political disturbance. At the beginning of the 19th century their activities were banned in Ireland. The movement is still in being.

Orvieto of Orvieto. The ancient walled cathedral city of Orvieto in Umbria, Central Italy, gives its name to the local white wine which has been sought by connoisseurs through centuries. The wine is named in 16th-century records. It is made in two types, dry and fruity, and both offer a limpid straw colour with a rare bouquet and a slightly bitter after-taste. A feature of the manufacture of Orvieto is the keeping of the wine in natural grottoes in the tufa rocks upon which the ancient city is built.

Ottoman Empire of Ottoman. The ottoman, an article of furniture much favoured in Victorian times, was properly a cushioned seat without back or arms and often with storing space under the lifting seat. The name also applied to sofas with arm and back, but generally with the distinctive storing space.

The name derived from the Turkish fashion in the Ottoman Empire whose power in Turkey was at its height in the 16th century. The name was taken from a warrior chief, Othman.

Oxford of Oxford Blue, Movement, bags, frames, etc. The University and cathedral city of Oxford, county town of Oxfordshire, has given its name to divers objects and activities.

The Oxford blue, a dark blue with an almost purple tinge, contrasts with the light blue of Cambridge University and is associated primarily in the public's mind with the classic Boat-race between the two great universities. The race, from Putney to Mortlake, was first held, at Henley, in 1829.

The Oxford Movement, or the Tractarian movement of last century, is regarded by many as the Catholic Revival within the Church of England. Many great men were associated with it and one of them, John Henry Newman (1801–90), dates the movement from the sermon of John Keble (1792–1866) at St. Mary's, Oxford, on July 14, 1833. It was a challenge to the government's abolition of ten Irish bishoprics.

Keble was a Fellow and Tutor of Oriel where Newman and Edward Pusey were also Fellows. The Movement insisted on the divine mission of the church and demanded a greater vigour in evangelization and mission work and a higher standard of clerical life and ceremonial. It revitalized and changed the whole face of the Anglican communion.

The Oxford Tracts, or *Tracts for the Times*, were the statements by the leaders of the Movement, published 1833–41.

The Oxford Group, a 20th-century religious movement founded by the American Dr. Frank Buchman (*b.* 1878) has no associations with the city and legal efforts have been made to prevent the use of the city's name and its implications in connection with this organization. The name was given to the Group by the South African press during a tour. Dr. Buchman was the instigator of Moral Rearmament.

Oxford bags were very wide flannel trousers, often in bright colours; a passing fashion affected by Oxford students for a period between the two world wars.

Oxford frames are the wooden picture frames constructed so that the sides cross at the corners and project beyond the dimensions of the glass. They are so named because the form has long been popular for the framing of college groups and other pictured activities of the university city.

Oxford mixture, or suiting, is a dark grey cloth and Oxford shoes, low-cut men's shoes laced over the instep.

The phrase "Oxford and Cambridge," embracing the two great senior universities, is used as a synonym of University education and pronouncements in a sense that is not applied to any other Universities in the British Isles.

The U.S. counterparts, and they comprise a phrase of similar application, are Harvard and Yale. The former was named after John Harvard (1607–38), who migrated as a Puritan minister to Charlestown, Mass., after taking a Cambridge degree.

Elihu Yale (1648–1721), was born in New Haven, Connecticut, and became Governor of Fort St. George, Madras.

Paisley of Paisley shawls, etc. The Roman town of Paisley is in Renfrewshire, seven miles from Glasgow. For several centuries it was noted for its shawls and distinctive weaving patterns. The popularity of the shawls has diminished in recent years, but the town supports many allied industries, such as linen, linen thread, bleaching and dyeing, etc. There are also substantial chemical, carpet and engineering works. Also shipbuilding as the town is on the White Cart, only a few miles above its junction with the Clyde.

Panama of Panama Canal, hat. Panama, the South American republic, was, prior to 1903, a department of the adjacent Colombia. The Isthmus of Panama joins North and South America and separates the Caribbean (Atlantic) from the Pacific Ocean.

The Panama Canal was designed in 1897 by Vicomte Ferdinand de Lesseps (1805–94). He had previously constructed the Suez Canal. The Panama Canal is 47 miles long, linking Colon with Panama City and running north-west to south-east.

Panama hats, of the typical fine and supple straw, are an export of the Panama district but appear originally to have been made principally in the adjacent southern republic of Equador. The straw is a product of the screw pine, the genus *Pandanus*, characterized by prickly leaves, spirally arranged and culminating in tufts similar to those of the pineapple.

Paris of Plaster of Paris, Paris doll, etc. The French capital gives its name to the fine, white plaster, used for making moulds and as cement, etc., because it was originally worked from gypsum in the famous Montmartre district to the north of Paris. It was and still is an artists' quarter whose residents found much use for the particular setting qualities of Plaster of Paris.

A Paris doll is the name given to a dressmaker's lay figure from its adoption and frequent use in the centre of Continental fashion.

The name of the French capital also appears in several colours, familiar and perhaps invented in its art circles: a pigment known as Paris blue; Paris white, a fine whiting used in polishing and burnishing; and Paris green, a pigment with poisonous qualities which account for its use also as an insecticide.

Parma of Parmesan, Parma violets. The ancient city of Parma, in Northern Italy, south-east of Milan, is the place of origin of parmesan, the popular Italian cheese now also made elsewhere. The dark green, or black, exterior is due to colouring matter rubbed on the surface. The green colouring of the cheese itself is attributed to discoloration by contamination from copper vessels used in its manufacture. The two chief types of the cheese are Parma and Reggian. The cheese is much favoured for soups, macaroni dishes and gnocchi.

Parma is a cathedral and university city, celebrated for its churches, many of which contain art treasures. Silk is manufactured there and there is a considerable trade in cattle, grain and produce.

The sweet-scented, lavender-hued Parma violet is associated with the city and district. (See *Naples— Neapolitan violet.*)

The apple, Worcester Pearmain, is thought to derive its last name from Parma.

The Pasquin of Pasquinade. The origin of pasquinade; the lampoon, political gibe, or local and often topical satire or ridicule, is authenticated. The Pasquin, pasquino, Pasquil or Pasquillo, as it was variously named, was a statue, excavated in a mutilated condition in the early 16th century, and erected in Rome near the Piazza Navoni. Most authorities attribute the discovery and re-erection of the statue near his palace to Cardinal Caraffa, of a distinguished Neapolitan family, one of whose members, Giovanni Pieto, became Pope Paul IV in 1555.

The statue is said to have been classical, but opinion was divided as to whether it had originally represented Ajax supporting Menelaus, other heroes or perhaps a gladiator.

The place of its re-erection was outside the house of one Pasquino, a local wit with a wide reputation for satire and personal ridicule. He is described as a tailor and a cobbler.

In the absence of sure identification of its subject the mutilated statue became known as the Pasquin, or Pasquil, and the local custom emerged of saluting the statue on St. Mark's Day (April 25) with Latin verses. The custom degenerated until the statue became the repository at all times for political gibes, personal satires and other often ribald comments and announcements that were more safely veiled in anonymity.

In another part of Rome a statue to Mars, called the Marforio, was used as the notice-board for replies and counter-retorts.

The statue and its derivative word are frequently mentioned in literature.

The street of the Governo, Pasquin's Street,
Where was stuck up, 'mid other epigrams,
A quatrain . . . but of all that, presently!
    Robert Browning (1812–89),
        The Ring and the Book.

Utter Pasquils, mere ribald libels on Humanity; these too, however, are at times worth reading.
    Thomas Carlyle (1795–1881),
        Count Cagliostro.

Peking of Pekinese. Peking, the ancient city of China was, until 1928, the capital. Here were bred the distinctive dogs with long silken hair which have become the most popular toy breed in Britain. They are noted for their courage and originality, coupled with a detached, almost haughty demeanour.

The breed is an ancient Chinese one and the dogs were until last century carefully raised and bred with zealous discrimination. They were court dogs and accorded deference. The finest animals were depicted on scrolls which later became known as the Imperial Books of Dogs. The Book constitutes a unique history in the annals of a particular breed.

The first Pekinese were brought to this country in 1860 and the breed gained prestige by the fact that Queen Victoria accepted one of the first arrivals.

Pembroke of Pembroke table, **College.** The seaport of Pembroke, in Pembrokeshire, Wales, on Milford Haven, gave its name to the distinctive form of table on four fixed legs with hinged flaps that can be extended and supported by fly brackets. Sheraton (1751–1806), who favoured the form, described the use of "this piece as for a lady or gentleman to breakfast on."

Some Pembroke tables, notably the Harlequin, embodied elaborate mechanical contrivances which this designer frequently utilized. The Harlequin included a nest of small drawers and pigeon-holes which could be raised from the table-top level to a height of twelve inches. He explained that it was so named because in Harlequin exhibitions "There is generally a great deal of machinery introduced in the scenery."

Pembroke College, Oxford, was founded in 1624 by James I and named in honour of the Earl of Pembroke, who was then Chancellor of the University. It was Dr. Johnson's College and his portrait by his friend,

Sir Joshua Reynolds, is at the College. Other famous names associated with Pembroke include Francis Beaumont, the dramatist, Sir Thomas Browne (*Religio Medici* and *Urn Burial*), Sir William Blackstone, the great legal authority, and George Whitefield, founder of the Calvinistic Methodists.

Le Perche of Percheron. The famous breed of horses known as Percherons were first raised in the French district of Perche, bounded on the north and west by Normandy. The breed was raised extensively for coach, post and artillery work in France. They won a considerable reputation in England. The breed is now raised extensively in the United States.

Persia (Iran) of Persian Carpets, cats, the Laws of the Medes and Persians. Persian art dates from 500 B.C. and is equally famous for pottery and carpets. The pottery is known primarily by collectors and connoisseurs; the carpets have achieved general recognition and public association with the country of their origin.

They are basically of two types, the *gelim*, or woven carpet, and the knotted type known as *quali*.

The carpets, which are nowadays made extensively by nomadic tribes, are distinguished by vivid colours and a luxurious finish. The traditional designs include gardens, hunting scenes and formal borders and medallions which often incorporate vases of traditional Persian design.

The Persian cat is distinguished by long, silky hair. It can be of a level silver shade with green eyes or a Blue Persian with amber eyes. Persian kittens are less playful than the young of other breeds.

The laws of the Medes and Persians were cited as the prototype of unalterable laws.

"Now, O King, establish the interdict, and sign the writing, that it be not changed, according to the law of the Medes and Persians, which altereth not" (*Daniel vi. 8*). "Let it be written among the laws of the Persians and the Medes, that it be not altered" (*Esther i. 19*).

The Medes inhabited Media, in ancient times the north-west part of Persia, with whose people they were closely allied in religion, law and language.

Peru of Peruvian Bark. The west South American republic of Peru is the home of the cinchona tree which grows extensively on the slopes of the Andes and also in India, Java and elsewhere.

The evergreen, flowering tree, of which there are many varieties, provides the well-known Peruvian bark. From it quinine and other alkaloid substances are obtained. Quinine is a noted specific for malaria and is a general febrifuge.

It is said to have been first used in this capacity in the 17th century to cure the fever of the Countess of Chinchon, wife of the ruler of Peru. Its success led to the wide distribution of the bark through Europe, largely by means of Jesuits, for which reason it was, and is still, also known as Jesuits' Bark.

Pharos of Pharos. The term Pharos can be applied to any lighthouse but derives from that built on the island of Pharos, off Alexandria, Egypt.

On the island, which Alexander connected with the mainland by a mole nearly a mile in length, Ptolemy the Second (Philadelphus, 285–246 B.C.) built the great Pharos. It was 450 ft. high and its light of fires or torches guided mariners to the harbours on the east of the mole. The light, which was said by historians to be visible for over 40 miles, was thought to be the first of its kind.

The Pharos was one of the Seven Wonders of the World.

Philippi of "Meet me at Philippi," etc. The use of the word Philippi in this and similar expressions threatening retribution, derives from the town of Macedonia. Here, in 42 B.C., Brutus and Cassius killed themselves after their forces had been routed by those of Antony and Octavian.

Brutus: Why com'st thou?
Ghost: To tell thee thou shalt see me at Philippi.
Brutus: Well; then I shall see thee again?
Ghost: Ay, at Philippi.
Julius Caesar, iv. 3.

At this town St. Paul founded a Christian colony in A.D. 53 and to its members he addressed his *Epistle to the Philippians.*

Philistia of the Philistines. The term Philistine has a much wider significance than its nominal application to a native of Philistia. The term as a synonym for the ignorant and uncultured is said to be primarily due to Matthew Arnold (1822–88), who introduced it in his *Essays in Criticism.* His source was said to have been the word *philister,* a term given to outsiders and aliens by the students of German universities.

The original Philistines were an alien, militant people of nomadic origin who harassed the Israelites. They are mentioned frequently in the Old Testament, were apparently uncircumcized and regarded as enemies by the Hebrews. Goliath was a Philistine, which people lived in or travelled from the lowland district of Philistia, in the Mediterranean coast between Jaffa and Gaza (*q.v.*). The principal administrative centres of the region were Gaza, Ashdod, Ekron and the frequently linked Gath and Askelon (*q.v.*).

Samson wrought havoc upon the Philistines, whose god was Dagon. At his death he pulled down the temple of Dagon on himself and the Philistines, more than 3,000 of whom were slain (*Judges xvi. 23–30*).

Pisgah of Pisgah promise, view, etc. The use of the word Pisgah in a phrase implying expectation, refers to Mount Pisgah, whence Moses viewed the Promised Land. It was a range in Moab, where Balak and Balaam sacrificed (*Num. xxiii. 14*).

The relative passage is *Deut. xxxiv. 1–4.* "And Moses went up . . . to the top of Pisgah . . . and the Lord shewed him all the land of Gilead, unto Dan; and all Naphtali, and the land of Ephrai, and Manasseh, and all the land of Judah, unto the hinder sea; and the South, and the Plain of the valley of Jericho the city of palm trees, unto Zoar. And the Lord said unto him, this is the land which I sware unto Abraham, unto Isaac, and unto Jacob, saying, I will give it unto thy seed: I have caused thee to see it with thine own eyes . . ."

Moses died at Pisgah and was buried in the valley, "but no man knoweth of his sepulchre unto this day" (*5–6*).

Plymouth of the Plymouth Brethren. Plymouth, the important Devon seaport and great naval harbour, was one of the originating places of the religious sect which became known, and is still known to those outside its organization, as the Plymouth Brethren. The members do not accept the name which arose from the sect's association with Plymouth although it was equally active in Dublin and elsewhere. The sect, which became prominent about 1830 and is now widely spread, was against formalism of any kind, particularly High Church teaching. It acknowledged no special ministers but accepted the right of all members to preach and testify.

Their alternative name of "Darbyites," now seldom heard, was not associated with the northern county town. It derived from one of the founders, a prominent solicitor named John Nelson Darby (1800–82).

The tenets of the sect, which has subdivided since its foundation, are largely Calvinistic.

Plymouth Rock is the name of a breed of large domestic fowl of American origin. Plymouth, Mass., south-east of Boston, was founded by the Pilgrim Fathers who settled there in 1620.

Poland of Polonaise. Poland, the birthplace of Chopin (1809–49), is the origin of the word polonaise, a stately native dance originally associated with ceremonial processions.

The music is generally in three-four time and the form of this and other folk dances was much favoured by Chopin and other composers.

A polonaise is also a woman's dress of bodice and skirt open from the waist downwards, which fashion also has Polish associations.

The sausage known as Polony is credited by some authorities with derivation from Poland; by others its origin is cited as the historic Italian cathedral and university city and province of Bologna (q.v.).

Polonium, the radio-active element, is so named from Poland, the country of its discoverers, M. and Mme Curie. It was the first radio-active substance to be recognized by them in 1898. It was detected in a combination of pitchblende.

Bologna of Polony. Bologna, the ancient cathedral and university city of northern Italy, is claimed by some as the place of origin of the once familiar polony, a large sausage consisting preferably of partially cooked pork. Other authorities trace the name from Poland, through the early Latin form, *Polonia*.

Polonius, whom the schoolboy described as "a mythical sausage," is Lord Chamberlain in *Hamlet*.

Pomerania of Pomeranian. Pomerania, the north-east, maritime province of Prussia, on the Baltic, claims to be the original breeding place of the Pomeranian dog, known in Britain as a toy variety. It has

declined in popularity during the present century.

The origins of the breed are northern or arctic and in Germany it was known as the Spitz, or Wolfspitz, a Pomeranian sheepdog. Its weight and size were then three or four times that of the eventual toy breed now achieved and favoured in this country.

The breed became popular here a century ago and public interest was increased by Queen Victoria's patronage.

Since about 1910 the Pomeranian has surrendered its supremacy in the world of toy dogs to the Pekinese (q.v.).

Pontefract of Pontefract or Pomfret Cakes. The liquorice lozenges, impressed with a castle, like a seal, are world-famous and are the product of the West Riding town of Pontefract, 13 miles south of Leeds.

The name of the town is still frequently referred to as Pomfret (*Pro. Pumfret*), a reversion to the ancient spelling of Pontfret. There are still ruins to be seen of the Norman castle. Malting and market gardening are staple industries.

Licorice, or liquorice, is extensively grown in Pontefract for the manufacture of the cakes. It is a perennial herbaceous plant, named *Glycyrrhiza glabra*, native to Southern Europe. It has bluish flowers and a substantial tap root which, when sliced and boiled, yields liquorice or "Spanish juice." It is manufactured in sticks as well as in the cakes and is used extensively in medicine for its pleasant taste and soothing qualities.

Poplar of Poplarism. The East London borough of Poplar had its name perpetuated in the word Poplarism, to denote a lavish expenditure of rates on out relief, or any other prodigal spending of rates. The occasion was the practice of the local Board of Guardians, just after the First World War, 1914–18.

Papal Avignon of Poplin. Avignon, the ancient city of Provence, was the original place of manufacture of poplin, the dress and upholstery fabric. Its characteristic is a corded structure achieved by a silk warp and a worsted weft.

It was so named from Papal (Fr. *popeline*) because Avignon was the seat of the Papacy during the 14th century and was for a longer period governed by a Papal Legate. Many relics of the Papal era remain and the city is still the seat of an archbishop.

The manufacture of poplin was introduced into England by Huguenot refugees. It is now chiefly manufactured in Ireland.

Oporto of Port Wine. Oporto, the cathedral city of Portugal, is also an important seaport, on the river Douro in the province of Minho. It is the centre of the port wine trade but sustains many other manufactures, including fabrics, hosiery, cutlery, glass, etc. It is a university city.

Port wine, which takes its name from the contraction of the city's name, is a wine fortified by the addition of spirit to control fermentation and retain the sweetness. It is made from vineyards on the banks of the Upper Douro and shipped from Oporto.

By Treaty between Portugal and Great Britain no other wine may be described as Port, though the terms such as "Port type," "Port style" are legitimately employed for wines produced elsewhere. The Spanish Tarragona is similar in character.

Port may be described as "Ruby," "Tawny" or "White." The last named is in fact of a pale yellow colour.

Claret is the liquor for boys; port for men;
but he who aspires to be a hero must drink brandy.

Dr. Johnson (1709–84).

Portland of Portland stone, cement, vase. The small Portland peninsula of Dorsetshire, connected with the mainland by the Chesil Bank, gives its name to the noted local stone.

Portland cement, so named because it was deemed to resemble Portland stone in colour and texture, was invented by a bricklayer, Joseph Aspdin, of Leeds, in 1824. It is an admixture of chalk and clay. It is manufactured extensively in many localities, particularly on the lower reaches of the Thames and the Kentish Medway.

The Peninsula contains an ancient fortress, a 16th-century castle and a noted convict prison.

The Portland Vase, an outstanding piece of Greek art, is a cinerary urn, about ten inches high, of dark blue transparent glass with superimposed figures in white relief. It was discovered in a Roman sarcophagus in the 17th century and was purchased by Sir William Hamilton in 1770. It came into the possession of the Duke of Portland who, in 1810, lent it to the British Museum, of which he was a trustee. It was smashed by a maniac in 1845 but has been skilfully repaired.

Purbeck of Purbeck Marble. The peninsula of Purbeck, Dorsetshire, lies west of Bournemouth and forms the southern arc of Poole harbour. Corfe Castle is in the centre of the area, which is traversed from east to west by the Purbeck chalk hills. The famous Purbeck marble is much used in ecclesiastical architecture and can be seen in Canterbury, Chichester and other cathedrals.

Cydonia of Quince. Cydonia, the district of ancient Crete, gives its name, through the Latin, to the tree and fruit known as the quince, or *Cydonia vulgaris*. The tree yields a large irregular, pear-shaped fruit, with a fragrant, almost aromatic scent but a bitter flavour. It is palatable mixed with apples, etc. Quince trees produce numerous fibrous surface roots and the stock is much favoured for grafting pears. The seeds, which adhere with an unusual mucus, are used medicinally.

Quince is the carpenter in *Midsummer Night's Dream*.

R

Reno of the Reno Divorce. Reno, the largest city of Nevada, U.S.A., has many claims to attention. It is surrounded by magnificent scenery, has a notable airport on the transcontinental air mail route, and an agricultural research station. The University was moved to Reno from Elko in 1873. Its chief claim to notoriety, however, is its divorce facilities. The State of Nevada requires only a short residence in order to qualify for divorce proceedings in its courts and the local laws give a wide range of grounds for an absolute decree. As a result, Reno has been called the Capital of Divorce, and many thousands of people "colonize" in the city each year to avail themselves of the unusual facilities.

The city is named after General Jesse Lee Reno (1823–62), a Federal Officer in the Civil War.

Ribston of Ribston Pippin. Ribston Park, in Yorkshire, is said to be the place of introduction of the pippin apple from Normandy at the beginning of the 18th century. Sir Henry Goodricke is credited with planting three pips, only one of which survived to become the progenitor of a now world-famous species.

Rollright of the Rollright Stones. The prehistoric circle known as the Rollright Stones is a miniature Stonehenge in the north-west corner of Oxfordshire, near the borders of Gloucestershire and Warwickshire.

The stones, set on an isolated ridge high above sea level, consist of a circle, some 100 ft. in diameter, an adjacent small group known as the Whispering Knights, and a solitary King's Stone to the north. Many prehistoric relics have been found in the parish, through which runs one of the most ancient roads in Britain.

Legend says that the leader and his advancing army—with plotting knights at the flank—were promised the kingdom if the leader fulfilled certain conditions and could see Long Compton, the village lying in the valley to the north. Many are the stories and equally varied the explanations as to why he failed and he and his hosts were turned to stone. Some authorities claim that the stones in the circle are both "male," upright stones, and "female," horizontal stones. The King's Stone is still over 8 ft. above ground, despite severe weathering. The group is protected by the Office of Works and attracts thousands of visitors annually.

The name Rollright, or Rowldrich in some records, comes from the containing parish of Little Rollright. Its tiny field-set church has traces of monastic architecture and two notable tombs. The parish has only twelve inhabitants. There is a larger and more distant parish of Great Rollright.

Roquefort of Roquefort Cheese. The French cheese, Roquefort, is named from its Gascony town of origin, some 60 miles south-east of Bordeaux. The cheese is similar to the English Stilton (*q.v.*) and is a soft rennet made principally from the milk of ewes, but that of cows and goats may be added. The mottled appearance is due to the presence of a penicillium ripening agent. The cheese has been famous for two centuries and its manufacture was originally the province solely of shepherds. Part of the process is the insertion of mould by bread-crumbs between the layers of curd and the curing or ripening is done in natural caves over a period of several months.

A U.S. Roquefort cheese is also subject to a similar ripening process in caves and in a disused coal-mine.

Roxburghe of Roxburghe book-binding and Club. The Scottish southern inland county of Roxburgh-shire is also known as Teviotdale. John Ker, third Duke of Roxburghe (1740–1804), perpetuated the place name in the Roxburghe Club and in the type of binding favoured by him and his fellow bibliophiles. His library was celebrated and its sale in 1812 was a literary event. Dr. T. F. Dibdin describes it as "a fight" and records that there were over 10,000 items.

The printing club, formed by Dibdin in that year, perpetuated the name and was occupied in the printing and binding of classical works. Its first president was Earl Spencer. The style of binding favoured included a plain leather spine with gilt lettering. The leaves were generally untrimmed.

Royston of Royston crow and "A Royston horse . . ." The Hertfordshire town of Royston, between Stevenage and Cambridge, derives its name of "Kingstown" from the patronage of King Stephen, who erected a cross there. The church dates from the 12th century.

The name Royston is given to a hooded or grey variety of crow, perhaps through its identification and classification by ornithologists in that town.

The saying "A Royston horse and a Cambridge Master of Arts give way to none" arose from local custom. The town was noted for malt, which was heavily loaded on horseback for London. This important traffic was given precedence on local roads just as the Cambridge dons were "given the wall" in the streets of Royston as an act of courteous deference.

Rubicon of Crossing the Rubicon. The expression, which denotes the taking of an irretrievable step, derives from the famous river in Italy which marked the boundary between Roman Italy and Cisalpine Gaul, a province administered by Julius Cæsar.

When Cæsar crossed the Rubicon in 49 B.C. it was tantamount to an invasion of the Republic and an automatic ultimatum. The crossing in fact precipitated the Civil War.

Rugby of Rugby Football. The Warwickshire town of Rugby, at the junction of the Swift and the Avon, is an important railway centre and the focus of much engineering, electrical and radio activity.

It is world-known, however, for its public school, founded in 1567. Dr. Thomas Arnold (1795–1842), one of its greatest headmasters, raised it to the first rank of public schools. He is one of the *Eminent Victorians* by Lytton Strachey (1880–1932). *Tom Brown's Schooldays* by Thomas Hughes (1822–96), who was educated under Arnold, gives a noted picture of conditions at that age.

The association of the school with Rugby football arose through a spontaneous action by a scholar. Prior to 1823 there were many individual codes which had little in common beyond the basic rule that the ball must never be carried or passed forward. In 1823, towards the close of an exasperating game which threatened to end in a draw, this cardinal principle was violated by a Rugby boy, named William Webb Ellis, who seized the ball and scored. His unorthodox action was immediately censured but as quickly caught on and flourished at Rugby, whence it spread. A tablet commemorates the historic occasion. Webb later became rector of St. Clement's Danes, in the Strand, London, where Dr. Samuel Johnson worshipped.

S

Sadler's Wells of Sadler's Wells. The phrase "Sadler's Wells" has in recent years become the automatic designation of British ballet with a completeness and implication of quality never before achieved.

The world success of the Sadler's Wells company and of its training school has been responsible for the placing in the vocabulary of millions of balletomanes of the name of the company's headquarters, the Sadler's Wells Theatre, in Islington, London. The original well had for many centuries a reputation for medicinal virtues. It once belonged to the monks of nearby Clerkenwell.

The work of a highway surveyor, named Sadler, in the reign of Charles II, led to the rediscovery of the well. The virtues of the waters were exploited and a "music house" built upon the site. It had a long record of success with theatrical and less orthodox entertainment ventures.

The present theatre, which is also used for opera, was erected in 1931. Just as Lilian Baylis is instantly associated with the Old Vic. (*q.v.*), so the name behind the inspiration and world success of Sadler's Wells is that of Ninette de Valois.

Salem of Salem. The name Salem, applied to a Nonconformist chapel, refers to Jerusalem, so named in *Heb. vii. 2.* "Then also King of Salem, which is, King of peace . . ." There are similar references in *Gen. xiv. 18* and *Ps. lxxvi. 2.*

Samaria of the Good Samaritan. Samaria, now known as Sebastieh, was a city and province in the centre of Palestine, between Galilee in the north and Judæa in the south. It had a Mediterranean seaboard. Philip is recorded as going to the city of Samaria, preaching and baptizing

(*Acts viii. 5–13*). Orthodox Jews did not consider Samaria as part of the Holy Land and made great detours to avoid it when passing from north to south. The Samaritans were their hated enemies, which gives added point to the parable of the Good Samaritan (*Luke x. 30–37*).

Christ, in instructing the disciples to go forth and preach, says "Go not into the way of the Gentiles, and into any city of the Samaritans enter ye not: but go rather to the lost sheep of the house of Israel" (*Matt. x. 5–6*).

Samoyed of Samoyed Dogs. The Samoyed tribes of nomadic Siberian Mongols are found along the Obi and Yenisei rivers. The white, Arctic breed of dog associated with the district is not unlike the chow chow (*q.v.*) to the layman. It is used for sled work, the herding of reindeer and as a guard dog. The Samoyed is one species of the Russian and Siberian Spitz breed.

It has proved popular in this country since the beginning of the century. In Britain's less severe climate the Samoyed grows a much more luxurious and refined coat.

Sandhurst of Sandhurst. The name Sandhurst is synonymous with military training from the presence two miles out of the Berkshire town of the Royal Military College. It is the regular army's "university" and provides general as well as military education.

The College was transferred to Sandhurst from Great Marlow in 1813. During the First World War the Staff College at Camberley, Surrey, was also taken over for cadet training and has continued in such activity.

West Point is the U.S. equivalent and the French military college of

St. Cyr, near Versailles, is equally well known. It was founded by Napoleon.

Sans Souci of Sans Souci. The phrase "Sans souci," meaning "Carefree and easy; no bother," is used by millions who do not realize that, though it is literal French, the phrase was coined by Frederick the Great for his home. The King, Frederick the Second of Prussia (1712–86), planned a retreat for his later years and "Sans Souci" was erected, partly from the King's plans, in 1745–7. It was intended to be a country box, one storey high, on a hill near Potsdam. There, after his wars were over, "The Philosopher of Sans Souci" spent many years of his life and entertained, and often differed with, many great contemporaries, including Voltaire.

Saratoga of Saratoga Trunk. The large, hold-all travelling trunk known as the Saratoga was named from Saratoga Springs, the U.S. health resort and spa. It is due north of Albany.

Sardinia of Sardine. The Mediterranean, Italian volcanic island of Sardinia, supports among its industries extensive tunny and sardine fisheries. The term sardine was originally applied to young Sardinian pilchards cured and packed in oil and widely exported. Later it included other small fish, similarly marketed and caught and exported extensively from Scandinavian countries. The Brittany and Cornish coasts also contribute to the industry.

The sardine stone referred to in *Rev. iv. 3* is not connected with Sardinia but was probably, as rendered in the Revised Version, a sardius, or sard (*q.v.*), one of the yellow cornelian group.

Sardis of Sard. The capital of the ancient kingdom of Lydia, and of the Roman and Byzantine province of Lydia, was Sardis. The country lay between the Ægean Sea and Mysia.

The sard, named therefrom, is a quartz gem of the carnelian group. Its colour varies from yellow to brown, due to the presence of iron oxide. The Sardius stone of Biblical reference is thought to refer to the cornelian.

The sardonyx has a white layer superimposed upon a black background. The form is much favoured to secure contrasts in the cutting of cameos.

Sargasso of Sargasso Sea. Sargasso, or gulf-weed, is a species of seaweed characterized by globular air vessels which cause the weed to float in masses, sometimes as large as islands. It is found in the Gulf Stream and particularly in the Sargasso Sea. This is part of the Atlantic ocean, between 40° and 70° W. and 20° and 35° N. The weed (*Sargassum bacciferum*) was recorded by Columbus in 1492.

Satsuma of Satsuma ware. The former Japanese province of Satsuma was on the south-west extremity of the island of Kyushu, due south of Nagasaki. It is now known as Kagoshima. The local pottery, still known as Satsuma ware, was noted for its characteristic cream colour.

Sauternes of Sauterne. The village or commune of Sauternes, which has given its name to a famous class of white or golden wines, lies south of the Bordeaux district. This and the adjacent communes are known as the Sauternes-Barsac districts. The most famous sauterne is Château Yquem.

Savile Row of Savile Row. The term "Savile Row," as the synonym of bespoke tailoring, gives a hallmark to the art which has for generations claimed world recognition.

The Row, which runs between and parallel with Regent Street and New Bond Street, London, W., is the centre of the finest tailoring craftsmen and of allied wool merchants.

The eastern side of Savile Row was built during the reign of George II (1683–1760) and so named in honour of Lady Dorothy Savile. She married Richard Boyle, Earl of Burlington, a keen student of architecture whose name is perpetuated in the adjacent Burlington Streets, Arcade and Burlington House. (See *Academy*.) The western side of the Row was then occupied by the stabling of the residences in Old Burlington Street.

Early in the 19th century James Poole, a tailor's apprentice from Baschurch, Salop, moved to London and set up business in Bloomsbury and later in Regent Street. In 1825 he took a house in Old Burlington Street and conducted business in the front parlour.

His fame grew and necessary extensions to his premises resulted in the opening of a main entrance in Savile Row. This was about 1860.

His reputation and the fashionable custom it attracted caused other first-class tailoring firms and ancillary trades to establish themselves in the area. Thus Savile Row, which had been in turn a fashionable residential area and later a kind of early Harley Street, occupied by doctors and surgeons, became the focus of the most exclusive tailors and wool merchants. This position it has maintained and enhanced during the 150 years through which the business of Henry Poole has been administered in family succession.

Savoy of Savoyard. A Savoyard is properly a native of the province of Savoy in south-east France. It has become generally applied in this country to actors and supporters of the famous Gilbert and Sullivan operas. They were written for Rupert D'Oyly Carte and the first, *Trial by Jury*, was produced in 1875. *The Pirates of Penzance* was produced at the Bijou Theatre, Paignton,

Devon, in 1879 and at the Opéra Comique in London in the following year.

The Savoy Theatre saw the production of *Iolanthe* in 1882 and thereafter became the home of Gilbert and Sullivan opera, presenting the triumphs of *The Mikado* (1885), *The Yeoman of the Guard* (1888), *The Gondoliers* (1889), etc.

The theatre, which lies between the Strand and the Thames Embankment, is near the Savoy Chapel, which is a survival of the days when the 13th-century Earl of Savoy and Richmond had his palace there.

The savoy, a species of cabbage with crinkled leaves, is named from the French province.

Saxony of Saxe and Saxe blue. The German state of Saxony is responsible for the name saxe, applied to a type of photographic paper first manufactured there. The same local association is responsible for saxony, a fine wool and cloth made from it. Saxe blue was a familiar colour for this product.

Scotland Yard of Scotland Yard. The term Scotland Yard is synonymous in Great Britain with police administration and criminal investigation. New Scotland Yard, on the north Thames Embankment, near the Houses of Parliament, is the headquarters of the Metropolitan Police and the C.I.D. It is so called because the previous headquarters were in Scotland Yard, off Whitehall, near Trafalgar Square. The street was claimed to be the site of a palace given by King Edgar to Kenneth II of Scotland when he came to pay homage, and subsequently used as headquarters by Scottish kings when visiting the English capital.

Sealyham of Sealyham Terriers. Sealyham is a village in west Wales where, about the middle of the 19th century, the now widely known breed of short-legged, fearless terriers was started, by a local sportsman named Captain John Tucker-Edwards.

It was probably the result of a cross between a Parson Jack Russell terrier and a short legged fox terrier type known locally at that time. The breed, first called the Sealy Ham Terrier, was popular before the breeder's death in 1891 and has since extended its popularity.

Seidlitz of Seidlitz Powder. The village spa of Seidlitz, in Bohemia, was noted for the effervescent and tonic effect of its waters. Seidlitz powders, in their famous blue and white papers, when mixed in water, produced the sparkling and cooling aperient effects of the natural water. The ingredients include tartrates of sodium and potassium, sodium bicarbonate and tartaric acid.

Selters of Seltzer Water. The Selters district of Germany, near Limburg and north of Wiesbaden and Frankfurt, possesses natural springs which provide the basis of Seltzer water, a widely used table water with medicinal properties. It is commended for sufferers from many liver complaints. The water is also manufactured artificially. Its chief ingredients are bicarbonates of calcium, magnesium and sodium, sulphate of potassium with aeration by means of carbon dioxide.

Ceylon of Serendipity. Horace Walpole (1717–97) coined the wholly delightful word "serendipity" to describe the pleasant faculty of making welcome but unexpected discoveries by accident.

He claimed that he coined it from the title of a fairy story, *The Three Princes of Serendip*, which was the ancient name for Ceylon. The heroes in the story possessed the gift so nominated by the social historian of the 18th century.

Seville of the Seville Orange. The south-west province of Spain, known as Seville, was formerly part of the province of Andalusia. Its capital of the same name is a university city and the seat of an archbishop. It is an important commercial port. A leading export is the noted bitter orange, favoured for the making of marmalade. The name derives from the Greek, through the Portuguese *marmelado*. There are various conflicting accounts of the origin of the use of the word for an orange preserve as marmelada, in Portugal and Brazil, applied to a preserve made from the quince, *marmelo*. The orange is *laranja* and marmalade *doce de laranja*. *Laranjada* is orangeade.

Some accounts claim that the English use of the word marmalade was originally due to mislabelling of orange preserve sent to Britain at the same time as quince preserves correctly named.

Sèvres of Sèvres ware. The French town of Sèvres, just south-west of Paris, has been noted for several centuries for its production of fine porcelain. Much of it is designed for ornamental as distinct from utilitarian purposes. The works were established in Valenciennes in the Department of Nord in the 18th century and were moved to Sèvres after a few years. They were later acquired by the State. In addition to porcelain, Sèvres is noted for mosaic, stained glass and allied products of a high standard of artistic craftsmanship. The town houses a notable museum of pottery and local products.

Châlons-sur-Marne of Shalloon. Châlons, the capital of the department of Marne, France, is situated on the river Marne, a hundred miles east of Paris. It dates back to Roman times and has been a strategic centre in many wars.

It was noted for a worsted cloth, known as shalloon, and used extensively for linings and as a dress material. It is mentioned by Chaucer (1340–1400). The industry has died in the place of its origin but the term persists and a similar cloth is manufactured elsewhere.

Shanghai of "to Shanghai." The Chinese city and port of Shanghai is responsible for the nautical slang term "to shanghai," which means to drug or intoxicate a sailor and ship him while he is unconscious. It also applied to the same treatment when meted out to forced labour on board ship. The system may have been first employed at the Chinese port, or become so prevalent there that it was automatically associated with Shanghai, even though it was practised elsewhere.

Shan-tung of Shantung. The maritime province of Shantung, North China, is flanked on its rocky eastern promontory by the Gulf of Pechili and the Yellow Sea. The capital is Tsi-nan and the province includes the sacred mountain, Tai. Confucius was a native of Shan-tung. The industries include minerals, rice, cotton, grain and the manufacture of the noted silk which bears the local name.

Shetland of Shetland wool, knitting, pony. The Shetland, or Zetland, group of islands lies off the north coast of Scotland, of which it forms a county. The islands number over a hundred, only about a quarter of which are inhabited.

The chief island is Mainland; its capital, Lerwick. The name of these bleak, rugged islands derives from an old Norse name, under which country's rule they remained until the reign of James III. There is limited agriculture, fishing, peat cutting and, as in the neighbouring Orkneys, a characteristic wool and knitting industry.

The small sheep of the Shetlands yield a fine wool, generally plucked by hand, and there is a considerable woollen trade, including gloves and shawls.

Much of the industry is still primi-tive in its simplicity, but revealing a high standard of inherited craftsmanship. The children are taught to practise knitting, or "macking" as it is locally called, from the age of four.

The wool is cleaned and treated with seal oil before combing. Knitting pouches are worn, the spinning-wheel is still used, and the islanders have their own picturesque vocabulary of knitting terms and phrases.

Until the First World War, Shetland garments were circular, without shoulder or arm-hole shape.

The characteristic of the Shetland shawl is its fine texture, and it is claimed that some can be passed through a wedding ring. The shawl is built from one corner of the lace edge and has neither cast-off nor cast-on edges.

The well-known Shetland pony; small, sturdy and shaggy to withstand the climate, flourishes when exported.

Shillelagh of Shillelagh. The Irish cudgel or bludgeon takes its name from the small town of Shillelagh, in Co. Wicklow, Eire. It is almost due east of the port of Arklow, on the south-east coast. The woods of the district were originally the source of supply of these weapons. Oak and blackthorn were the most used timber.

Shirley of Shirley Poppy. The Croydon, Surrey, district of Shirley became an ecclesiastical parish in 1846. The Shirley poppy was produced by the Rev. William Wilks, a curate of Croydon and subsequently Vicar of Shirley from 1897–1912. It was first grown in the vicarage garden.

The Rev. William Wilks was a noted horticulturist, a member of the Floral Committee of the Royal Horticultural Society. He was elected to the Council and was Honorary Secretary for many years.

Siam of Siamese Twins, Cats. Siam, the kingdom in the Indo-Chinese peninsula, is chiefly connected in the

public mind with the physical pheno-
menon known as Siamese Twins.
The term is used in extension to
inseparables and mental and physical
affinities.

The original Siamese Twins were
Chang and Eng, who were born
about 1811 and discovered in adoles-
cence in Mekong, near Bangkok,
Siam. They were joined by a flexible
band between the breastbones. They
were commercially exploited and exhibited by, among others, the great
Barnum. They each married and
had between them twenty-two children, all intelligent and normal
physically, with the exception of two
deaf mutes. The parents of the
Siamese Twins were thought to have
been a Chinese father and a half-
Chinese mother.

Chang died at sixty-three, and
Eng two hours afterwards.

There have been a number of instances of "Siamese twins" born
subsequently and there have been
cases of successful separation either at
birth or later from the living or dead
partner. The physical link has varied
in different cases.

The Siamese cat, with certain dog-
like characteristics and a "bark"
rather than a mew, is short-haired,
cream-coloured with black or brown
markings. It is sometimes distinguished by its blue, "squinting" eyes
and a kink in its tail, though these
former characteristics are now less
evident.

Siena of Burnt sienna. The Tuscan
province of Siena, or Sienna, lies on
the west coast of Italy. Its capital of
the same name is the seat of an archbishop and a university city.

The pigments raw and burnt sienna
were originally obtained from ochrous
earth of the district, used either raw
as a brownish yellow, or burnt to a
reddish brown. The terms are used
also for similar colours not necessarily obtained from use of the pigments which were favoured by many
of the Italian masters.

Silverstone of Silverstone. Silverstone, near Kettering, Northants, has
become a household word since the
Second World War because of its
Royal Automobile Club motoring
race track there, the road which
skirts a disused aerodrome.

Its increasing prominence as a
racing centre was given international
significance in 1950 when the First
Grand Prix of Europe ever to be held
in the British Isles was staged at Silverstone in May, in the presence of
the King and Queen.

The sport had been hitherto handicapped in Britain by laws which prevented road racing. The premier,
international events were therefore
held in the Isle of Man, Northern
Ireland, the Channel Islands and, pre-
dominantly, on the Continent. The
French instituted the Grand Prix at
the beginning of this century. The
event, which attracts a crowd of over
100,000 spectators, is of high international value to the trade and win-
ning manufacturers.

Sisal of Sisal grass, hemp, etc. The
port of Sisal, in Yucatan, the south-
east Mexican peninsula, has given its
name to the fibre obtained from the
species of American aloe known as
Agave sisalana. Although the tree is
found also in other parts of Mexico, in
Florida, and has been successfully
planted in the West Indies, the Sisal
district produces the bulk of the
world's supply of the hemp.

The aloe, a genus of succulent
shrubs and trees, provides in the
expressed juice of its leaves an ingredient much used in medicine and
veterinary practice. Its wood is
fragrant, especially when burned.
Egyptians used aloes for embalming
and Nicodemus brought myrrh and
aloes to embalm the body of Christ
(*John xix. 39*).

The American species, which is
vulnerable to frost, has narrow, thick
leaves attaining a length of several
feet. The flesh of the leaves is
removed by machinery and the

strong, straight fibre remaining is made into rope and cord. The product is also known as henequen.

The Yucca, or Adam's Needle, a tropical evergreen shrub which can be seen in this country, is a native of the Yucatan region.

Skye of Skye terrier. The Inner Hebrides island of Skye, Inverness-shire, Scotland, gave its name to a breed of Scottish terriers which is less prominent under that name to-day. The breed, thought to be several centuries old, was originally sustained for the destruction of vermin and is still expert at badger hunting. The breed, made popular by the patronage of Queen Victoria, is now largely merged, at least in popular acceptance, with the more generally known Cairn terrier.

Sleepy Hollow of Sleepy Hollow. The term Sleepy Hollow is used by many without knowledge of its creator, to describe any somnolent backwater, hamlet or even particular residence.

The phrase was coined by Washington Irving (1783–1859) and used in his *The Sketch Book* (1819) to describe a peaceful, old-world village on the river Hudson. Its full title is *The Sketch Book of Geoffrey Crayon, Gent.*, and its most famous papers are *Rip Van Winkle* and *The Legend of Sleepy Hollow*.

Smithfield of Smithfield Market. The name Smithfield is synonymous with meat marketing, as Covent Garden Market is automatically linked with the distribution of fruit and vegetables. The district lies north of St. Paul's Cathedral, London, and since 1868 has been the province of the Central Meat Market.

The site has been a public ground, of varying fame and notoriety, since the 12th century. It was used for trials, executions, tournaments and fairs. The adjacent Giltspur Street is an echo of the Smithfield jousts.

Wat Tyler was executed there by Sir William Walworth in the presence of Richard II and there were Protestant martyrdoms at Smithfield during the reign of Queen Mary.

Smithfield, or Smooth Field, accommodated the famous Bartholomew's Fair, which continued until the middle of the 19th century. It became a great Cloth Fair and attracted many cattle dealers. For centuries it received civic recognition and was opened by the Lord Mayor. It continued to enjoy the reading of a proclamation until 1817.

In 1855 it had so deteriorated in character that it was suppressed as a public nuisance. The Fair is frequently mentioned in literature, from Ben Jonson onwards.

A century ago the Cattle Market was removed to Islington, North London, leaving Smithfield to deal with meat. Since then the Market has developed to include poultry, provisions, fish, greengrocery, etc. The premises, which occupy several acres, suffered severe bomb damage during the Second World War.

St. Bartholomew the Great, Smithfield, one of London's oldest and most famous churches, together with the adjacent "St. Bart's" Hospital, sprang from the 12th-century foundation of the monastery by Rahere, a former court Jester. He returned in pious mood from a pilgrimage to the Holy Land, obtained a royal grant of the land and proceeded to erect the monastery, church and hospital.

Sodom and Gomorrah, the cities of desolation and iniquity, etc. The cursed cities of Biblical days are still cited as synonyms of centres of iniquity and damnation.

Sodom, which means *burning*, was one of the five "cities of the plain," at the south end of the Dead Sea. Abraham pleads that if there be found even ten righteous men there, the city shall be saved from destruction (*Gen. xviii. 32*). The city is destroyed (*Gen. xix. 24*) when "the

Lord rained upon Sodom and upon Gomorrah brimstone and fire from the Lord out of heaven." The smoke of the country went up as the smoke of a furnace.

The name persists in the words "sodomy" and "sodomite."

The Apples of Sodom, or Dead Sea Apples, were fruit said to grow on the shores of the Dead Sea which, despite their alluring appearance, were found when eaten to be full of ashes. They were associated with Sodom probably to indicate the disaster of accepting the outward lure of the city's iniquity. Possibly the growth was the gall nut, produced by a parasite.

Gomorrah, another of the cities of the plain which shared the destruction of Sodom, was proverbial for its wickedness: "their grapes are grapes of gall, their clusters are bitter: their wine is the poison of dragons, and the cruel venom of asps" (*Deut. xxxii. 32–3*) and (*Jer. xxiii. 14*).

Christ cites the wickedness of these cities when instructing the disciples to go out after the lost sheep of the house of Israel. "And whosoever shall not receive you, nor hear your words, when ye depart out of that house or city, shake off the dust of your feet. Verily I say unto you, It shall be more tolerable for the land of Sodom and Gomorrah in the day of judgment, than for that city" (*Matt. x. 14–15*).

Soho of Soho. The London district of Soho, which lies between Oxford Street and Shaftesbury Avenue, bounded on the east by Charing Cross Road, is famous for its numerous foreign restaurants and eating houses. Many are frequented by connoisseurs and as many offer Continental, Oriental and other food and cooking for modest purses. The word Soho is synonymous with good wining and dining, often in picturesque surroundings.

Soho Square was formerly a fashionable quarter. Dryden and Evelyn are associated with it; Hazlitt died there. In recent times J. L. Baird conducted some of the vital first experiments with television in a garret in Frith Street.

The Square's foreign element dates from the 17th century when many Protestant refugees colonized there. It was first known as King's Square, after the builder.

St. Patrick's Roman Catholic church now occupies the site of a gaming house and such is the cosmopolitan population of its parish that sermons are preached there in as many as nine tongues.

The name is variously attributed to the battle cry of a 17th-century Duke of Monmouth and to the name of a mansion in the district known before his time, but perhaps occupied by him.

The term is used as a call in hare coursing, when the hare is "started," corresponding to the "Tally Ho!" of fox-hunting.

Spain of Spaniel, Spanish chestnut, fly, Main, etc. Spain appears in its adjectival form in many names, the association of which with the country is seldom understood.

The dog family of Spaniels, which embraces setters and retrievers, and includes breeds indigenous to many countries of the world, took its name from Spain, through *español*. The Spanish breed, famous for centuries, was a field dog, approximating to the Pointer of to-day.

The Spanish Chestnut, *Castanea Sativa*, is the sweet chestnut, not the Horse Chestnut or "conker" tree beloved of children. Though associated with Spain it is thought to have originated in Asia Minor and Greece and to have been brought to Britain by the Romans.

The Spanish fly, or Cantharidæ, which is found in Spain, France and other European countries, is known also as the blister beetle. The fly, of which there are winged and wingless varieties, is less than an inch in length, has a vivid green colour and raises blisters when in contact with the skin of animals, etc. When touched it feigns death and emits a sharp smell.

The drug, cantharides, which has blistering properties, is prepared from the dried Spanish fly, *Cantharidae vesticatoria.*

The Spanish Main, setting of many historical romances and songs, etc., was the popular description of the Caribbean Sea and the north coast of South America from Orinoco to Darien. The term embraced also the shores of the Spanish possessions in Central America. Dr. Alfred Noyes (*b.* 1880), in *The Moon is Up*, makes Drake say:

> "*We're out to seek a Realm of Gold,*
> *Beyond the Spanish Main.*"

The adjective Spanish is also applied to several pigments, esparto grass, a domestic fowl with glossy, greenish-black plumage, etc.

To "build castles in Spain" is to indulge in airy daydreams. There are similar expressions naming other countries and cities.

Sparta of Spartan. Sparta, or Lacedaemon, was the capital of Laconia, a state founded by the Dorians in the Peloponnese. The name was applied both to the city and the city-state of ancient Greece. The Spartans were conquerors and military rulers, less noted for commerce and art, though in the 7th century Sparta was the centre of choral lyric. The adjective "spartan," implying rigid discipline and hard living, derives, particularly as applied to mothers, from the harsh rules of Sparta, whereby weaklings were exposed and all children graduated through ascetic discipline and gymnastic training, to which intellectual instruction was subordinated. Spartan men were subject to barracks and rigid training until they were thirty and most aspects of their lives were controlled by the State, whose chief aim was the production of the mightiest army in Greece.

St. Andrews of St. Andrews. The royal burgh and university town of St. Andrews, Fifeshire, Scotland, is largely to golf what Lord's is to cricket and Wimbledon to tennis. The Royal and Ancient Golf Club of St. Andrews is the most famous in the world. It is the governing body whose decisions are recognized everywhere with the exception of the United States of America. It has had many royal captains and gathered much history since its foundation in 1754.

The links are known to have been in existence since the 15th century and there are surviving documents conveying certain rights in them in the 16th century. The course, once owned for a short period by the Club, has been for some years owned by the Corporation, by special Act of Parliament. It is administered by a committee which includes members of the Royal and Ancient, a title bestowed upon the Club by William IV.

Some half-dozen clubs can claim an even earlier foundation, but such is the fame of St. Andrews, which is the scene of many championships and international contests, that American visitors to London have been known to fly there and back in a day for the expensive privilege of playing half a round on the classic course.

St. Bernard's Hospice of the St. Bernard Dogs. The famous Hospice, built 8,000 ft. above sea-level on a pass between Switzerland and Italy, perpetuates the name of St. Bernard who was born in the Savoy in the 10th century.

He converted the hitherto murderous inhabitants of the pass and built the Hospice for travellers.

The monks who staff the Hospice are Canons Regular of the Order of St. Augustine and only the strongest can survive the severe conditions, and then only for limited periods. In addition to succouring the travellers they pursue classical and scientific studies.

Their famous dogs, many of which are capable of carrying a man, are a cross between a bulldog and a Pyrenean shepherd's dog. The breed has been maintained for four centuries.

Steinkirk of Steenkirk. The Belgian village of Steinkirk, spelt also Steenkirk and Steenkerque, was the scene, in 1692, of the defeat of the Allies by the French. The village is on the Seine, north-east of Mons. It gave its name to a cravat fashionable at the time and to other small articles of contemporary dress.

Stellenbosch of "to Stellenbosch." The South African town of Stellenbosch, east of Cape Town, gave its name to a military slang phrase, "to Stellenbosch," meaning polite supersession without formal disgrace. Many displacements rightly or wrongly judged to be in this category were achieved by appointments to unimportant or sinecure commands at the military base at Stellenbosch.

Stepney Street, Llanelly of the Stepney Spare Wheel. The main shopping thoroughfare of Llanelly, Carmarthenshire, is named Stepney Street after the Stepney family, large property owners in the district and local benefactors. Llanelly is a coal-mining seaport, north-west of Swansea.

It was there that the Stepney Spare Wheel was first and is still manufactured.

The fitting of the wheel, over the deflated car tyre, is a motoring boon which has achieved world-wide acceptance. The temporary wheel has done a 500-mile run without damage to the deflated tyre. The Stepney wheel carries the same size tyre and tube as is used in the basic fitting, so that motorists can use their own spares on the Stepney, which is always ready for use and can be placed in position in a couple of minutes.

The wheel was first made at the rear of the Stepney Street ironmonger's shop of T. Morris Davies and his brother, Walter Davies.

The former, who had already revealed inventive ability, was particularly stung by the caustic remarks of a judge at Brecon Assizes when two Llanelly men arrived late at court. The cause was a tyre burst on the car in which Mr. Davies was driving them and the judge deplored the unreliability of motor transport.

The Stepney wheel was eventually evolved and patented in 1904. It received the usual adverse criticisms and negative reception and at one time the brothers were prepared to sell the device for £3,000. When it proved itself all over the world, in all conditions, they were paid £70,000 for it. Improvements and developments followed and the Stepney is now the basis of a flourishing industry. The Stepney bicycle is also a product of the company.

Stilton of Stilton Cheese. The Huntingdonshire village of Stilton, a few miles south-west of Peterborough, is not the home of the famous English cheese so named. It was and is made in Leicestershire. But it was first served in the famous Bell Inn at Stilton, always noted for good fare. Its notable copper sign, the massive Tudor windows and the ancient archway leading to the stable yard make the Bell one of the most historic inns in Britain and a pageant of history must have passed before its sign upon the Great North Road.

Stockholm of Stockholm tar. The capital of Sweden, Stockholm, gave its name to the special tar, prepared from resinous pinewood, which is used extensively in ship building.

The city and port, which is built on the mainland and adjacent islands, has a great harbour, cleared in winter by ice-breakers. It supports extensive shipbuilding, engineering and allied industries.

Conestoga of Stogy. The crude, heavy boot or shoe, known as the stogy or stogie, is named from a contraction of Conestoga, a town in Pennsylvania, U.S.A.

The name stogy is also given to a crudely fashioned cigar.

Stonesfield of Stonesfield Tiles. The hand-wrought Stonesfield tiles which are a feature of Cotswold architecture, take their name from the village of Stonesfield, a few miles west of Woodstock, in central Oxfordshire. The grey sandstone which comes from the local quarries has contributed much to the beauty of the county's architecture and is seen in many colleges and churches.

The quarries, which were worked by the Romans, have also produced a remarkable collection of fossils of great antiquity.

Stymphalus of the Stymphalian Birds. The Stymphalian birds of mythology took their name from Lake Stymphalus, a mountain-locked waterway against Mount Cyllene, in north Arcadia (*q.v.*). It was spring fed and laced with chasms and underground caves.

The terrifying birds lived in the surrounding woods and infested Arcadia. Their wings, claws and beaks were brazen, they used their feathers as arrows and fed upon human flesh. The strength of their terror is indicated by the fact that their extermination was one of the twelve labours of Hercules. He killed many and scattered the rest with his brazen rattle. Some returned in later times and their presence is recorded in the history of the Argonauts.

The Styx of "Crossing the Styx," Stygian. The river Styx "the abhorrent," was, in Greek mythology, the principal river of the underworld. Milton (1608–74) calls it "the flood of burning hate." It was said to encompass the infernal regions seven or nine times.

Charon was the squalid ferryman who conveyed the dead across the river. His fee was an obol, and to pay it the dead were buried with a small coin in their mouths. Charon is mentioned by Virgil and Aristophanes.

The derivative adjective, Stygian, means of the Styx or of Hades; murky, gloomy, infernal.

Suffolk of Suffolk Punch. The east midland, maritime county of Suffolk gives its name to a famous breed of short-legged, thick-set draught horse, known as the Punch. It is one of the finest shire horses and the breed can be traced from about 1760. The colour is chestnut and the Punch is noted for its strength and gentleness. It is claimed that a child can lead the greatest Suffolk stallion without fear.

The phrase "Suffolk Punch" is also used locally to describe a short, thick-set person or object.

The epithet "Silly Suffolk" derives from the early nickname for the county, "Selig," a Saxon word meaning Blessed or Holy. The county is noted for magnificent churches, many of them associated with the days when Suffolk was the centre of a prosperous weaving industry, implemented at different times by Flemish and Huguenot settlers.

Surrey of the Surrey carriage. The southern English home county of Surrey gave its name to the light, two-wheeled carriage popular in the 19th century, probably owing to its being favoured by society in the fashionable centres of the county.

Switzerland of the Swiss Guards. Apart from the now widely made cake, the Swiss roll, the name of Switzerland is chiefly remembered, outside local associations, by the Swiss Guard. This famous regiment of mercenaries was formed in the French army in the 17th century. They still form, picturesquely dressed, the Pope's escort at the Vatican.

The men, who are recruited from each canton of Switzerland, are not to be confused with His Holiness's Papal Guard.

Sybaris of Sybarites, Sybaritic. The ancient Greek colony of Sybaris was on the Gulf of Tarentum, in Southern Italy. It flourished in the 7th century B.C. but in 500 B.C. was overrun by the rival colonists of Crotonia.

A legend has it that the Sybarites taught their horses to dance to the pipes, and this local knowledge was exploited by the invading Crotonians who advanced playing pipes and benefited by the resulting confusion when the enemy's horses suitably responded.

The fabulous luxury and voluptuousness of the Sybarite colony was known throughout the ancient world. One of them is said to have complained of a sleepless night and discovered a rose petal doubled under him.

The name became synonymous with excessive luxury and sensuousness and to some extent with effeminacy and wantonness.

Tanagra of **Tanagra**. The name tanagra, applied to statuettes, particularly of terra cotta, derives from Tanagra, the city of ancient Greece, in Bœotia, near Thebes. Earthenware statuettes found on the site of the city are regarded as among the finest Greek craftsmanship in this medium.

Tangier of **Tangerine**. Tangier, or Tangiers, is the largest commercial city of Morocco, and its administrative headquarters. It is a seaport on the bay of the Strait of Gibraltar.

Tangier was under British control from 1662–84, when it formed part of the dowry of Catherine of Braganza. Legislation is now in the hands of an international assembly. There is a small British colony.

Market gardens are among the many industries of Tangiers, which gives its name to the small, flattened orange, known as the tangerine.

The similar mandarin, or manderine, is thought to have derived its name from the mandarin, perhaps owing to the orange colour of that official's robes. The word is not Chinese, but of Portuguese origin.

Taranto of **Tarantula, Tarantism, Tarantella**. The fortified town and seaport of Taranto (Tarentum), in Southern Italy gives its name to a species of hairy spider found in Europe and America. The spiders are large, formidable-looking and have a poisonous bite, though not one calculated to produce the extreme symptoms associated with tarantism.

This dancing mania, known also as Tarantulism, became epidemic in Italy in the 16th and 17th centuries. It was accompanied by hysteria and arose not from the bite of the spider but from mass fear thereof. The disease spread to other parts of Europe.

The Tarantella, the rapid, swirling Italian dance (or its music) derives its name from the same source.

It is variously held to be based on the agitated movements of those afflicted by the bite of the tarantula, on the movements of those suffering from tarantism, and to derive from a dance which was originally a cure for the real or imagined disease.

Tasmania of **Tasmanian Devil, etc.** Tasmania, the seventh state of the Australian Commonwealth, separated from the continent by the Bass Strait, was named after its Dutch discoverer, Abel Janszoon Tasman (c. 1601–59).

The country has given its name to the Tasmanian Devil, a ferocious, cat-like carnivorous marsupial peculiar to the island and to certain adjacent parts of Australia. It is also known as the dasyure, a word of Greek derivation meaning "rough tail." In appearance it is something like a small bear, brownish-black and with a long tail. It has a broad pectoral band of white. The animal will raid and destroy poultry and attack even sheep.

The Tasmanian wolf is a local carnivorous marsupial.

Telemark of **Telemark**. The Norwegian district of Telemark has given its name to the expert skiing movement, a swinging turn employed to change direction or to stop abruptly.

Terai of the **Terai**. The wide-brimmed felt hat, often distinguished by a double crown and worn by white men in sub-tropical and tropical regions, is named from the Terai, or Tarai, a tract of unhealthy marshy jungle-land in the Kumaun district of India. It lies between the Himalayan foothills and the plains.

Timbuktu of "He's gone to Timbuktu," etc. Timbuktu, also spelt Timbucktoo, Timbouctou, etc., is a town with a population of some 7,000 in French Sudan, near the Sahara. It is 9 miles from the Niger and is a centre of many caravan routes between Algeria, Morocco and the Guinea Coast. Though many of the buildings are primitive, the place is fortified and is responsible for much trade. It was formerly a military territory but was converted to a civil administration under a lieutenant-governor in 1923.

Its comparative remoteness and perhaps its picturesque name have caused it to be used in phrases which imply an unknown and unpredictable destination. (See *Jericho*.)

Tokay of Tokay. Tokay is a small north Hungarian town whose famous wines come from vineyards on a mountain plateau. The two chief varieties, cherished by connoisseurs, are Imperial Tokay and Szanorodner. The former is the produce of the once Royal vineyards; the latter is of a drier, more hock-like character.

Toledo of Toledo Swords. The rugged, granite city of Toledo is capital of the Spanish province of the same name and was once capital of Spain. It is south-south-west of Madrid, on the Tagus. It is world famous for its swords, which have been cited as the perfection of craftsmanship for over 2,000 years. They are made by private firms and in the Royal factory. The industry reached its peak under the Moors. The steel is so finely tempered that it is claimed that the swords can be curled up like watch springs.

> *The trenchant blade Toledo trusty.*
> Samuel Butler (1612–80), *Hudibras.*

Toledo was the Toletum of the Romans. It was the headquarters of the Inquisition.

Tolpuddle of The Tolpuddle Martyrs. The quiet Dorset village of Tolpuddle, Dorset, 7 miles east-north-east of Dorchester, would seem to be the most unlikely setting for a violent crisis in the early struggle for fair working conditions for British agricultural labour.

Yet here, in 1830, six labourers, of whom the brothers George and Joseph Loveless were the most prominent, unwittingly drew world attention to their tragic plight.

They sought to resist the reduction of Dorset wages from 7*s.* to 6*s.* a week. They and four others were charged with conspiracy but insisted that if they had violated any law it was unconsciously, for they sought only to preserve themselves, their wives and children from utter degradation and starvation.

The trial and conviction were smeared with class prejudice, in contrast with which the demeanour of the God-fearing, earnest men made a deep impression.

The sentence at the Spring Assizes in Dorchester, 1834, to seven years' transportation in chains to Australia, aroused violent public disgust. The pardon of the prisoners was demanded and secured, but the conditions of release were complied with so tardily and so underhandedly that they added to the legal and administrative disgrace of the occasion.

In 1934 six cottages were set up in Tolpuddle by the Trades Union Congress as a memorial to the Tolpuddle Martyrs and the buildings handed over to the National Trust.

There is a Memorial Chapel and the tree under which the men met still stands in the village green.

Tooley Street of The Three Tailors of Tooley Street. The name of the Southwark Street, near London Bridge, is a corruption of St. Olaf, through 'T-Olaf, Tolay. Tradition claims that three tailors of the street presented a petition to the House of Commons in the 18th century opening with the words, "We, the people of England . . ." Canning is claimed to have cited them.

The phrase still has literary currency to apply to similar presumption.

Troy of "To work like a Trojan," etc. Troy was a city of Troas, northwest of Mysia in Asia Minor. Its citizens are cited as the prototypes of prodigious workmen of unremitting courage and with a highly developed sense of citizenship.

The Trojan War, waged by the Greeks for some ten years against Troy, is described in the *Iliad* of Homer. The burning of Troy is described by Virgil in the *Aeneid*.

The wooden horse of Troy, which phrase is applied to many a courageous, deceptive ruse, was a huge horse hauled into Troy and purporting to be an offering to the gods. It was full of Grecian soldiers who, at night, revealed themselves, slew the guards and opened the gates of the city to secure its destruction by fire.

A wooden horse, in this case a vaulting-horse, was the means of one of the epic escapes of British prisoners during the Second World War.

The supremely beautiful Helen of Troy, whose title is still used as a synonym of outstanding female attraction, eloped with Paris to Troy and thus brought about the siege. Pope's translation of the *Iliad* says of her: "She moves a goddess and she looks a queen."

The comment of Pascal (1623–62) that if her nose had been shorter the whole face of the earth might have been changed did not refer to Helen, as many believe, but to Cleopatra.

Of Helen it was said by Marlowe (1564–93) in *The Tragedy of Dr. Faustus. Scene xiv*:

Was this the face that launched a thousand ships
And burnt the topless towers of Ilium?
Sweet Helen, make me immortal with a kiss.

Troy weight, used for gold and silver and drugs, is not named after the ancient city but probably derives from usage at the French cathedral city of Troyes, in the department of Aube. It was one of the richest cities in Champagne and noted for its commercial fairs. The weight has been recognized since the 15th century. The Troy pound contains 5,670 grains; 24 to the pennyweight and 20 pennyweights to the ounce.

For drugs and other medicines the Troy table is:

20 grains	=	1 scruple
3 scruples	=	1 drachm
8 drachms	=	1 ounce
12 ounces	=	1 pound

Tulle of Tulle. The fine silk net material used for veils, etc., is named from Tulle, capital of the Department of Correze, in south central France. It is part of the old province of Limousin (*q.v.*). To-day the most important manufacture of the district is firearms and ammunition.

Turkey of Turkey carpets. Turkey, the former Ottoman Empire, has been famous for centuries for its rich carpets, not dissimilar from the Persian product (*q.v.*). The designs are generally more formal. Uskah was the chief centre of manufacture but the type of carpet was introduced into Axminster and Wilton (*qq.v.*) in the 18th century.

Tuxedo of Tuxedo. The name Tuxedo for the U.S. dinner jacket, derives from the town of the same name in Orange County, New York. It is some 40 miles north-north-west of New York City. At the beginning of the 19th century a vast tract of land, including lakes, was taken in settlement of a debt. Shooting rights were developed and the grandson of the owner, named Lorillard, formed the Tuxedo Park Association. From this sprang the noted Tuxedo Park and the Tuxedo Club (1886). It became a fashionable social centre and the widely used dinner jacket was associated with it.

Tweed of Tweed. The river Tweed in southern Scotland ran through many districts where the woollen cloth was manufactured, but the name is said to have been originally *twill*, or *tweel*, meaning two-thread, the association with the extensive manufacture on the banks of the Tweed led to the gradual change of name. (See *Harris*.)

Twickenham of Twickenham. The Middlesex borough of Twickenham, on the left bank of the Thames, opposite Richmond, is synonymous in the public mind with Rugby Football. It is to the sport what Wimbledon is to tennis and Lord's to cricket.

This identification arises from the site there of the Rugby Union's famous ground on which are played internationals, inter-University matches and representative matches with all the famous touring sides that visit this country. The ground was purchased in 1907.

Twickenham had previously many literary associations. Many celebrities lived there, particularly in the neighbourhood of Strawberry Hill. They included Pope, Sir Godfrey Kneller and Horace Walpole. The first named was known as "The Bard of Twickenham," from his long residence.

U

Ulster of the Ulster, Ulster King of Arms. Ulster, Northern Ireland, gave its name to the long, loose overcoat generally belted, because the belt was made originally of Ulster frieze, a coarse woollen cloth with a nap on one side.

The Ulster King of Arms is the chief heraldic officer in Ireland and Registrar of the Most Illustrious Order of St. Patrick. The office does not come under the jurisdiction of the London College of Arms. The Ulster King of Arms has offices at Dublin and Heralds at Dublin and Cork.

The English Kings of Arms are Garter, Clarenceaux, and Norroy.

The Heralds are Windsor, Chester, Richmond, Somerset, York and Lancaster; the pursuivants, Rouge Croix, Bluemantle, Rouge Dragon and Portcullis.

The chief Herald in Scotland is the Lyon King of Arms, so named from the lion on the Royal shield.

V

Valencia of Valencia, V. almonds, etc. Valencia, the maritime province and former kingdom of Eastern Spain, supports a large textile industry.

Valencias, local fabrics, were generally striped and characterized by a wool weft with a warp of silk, cotton or other contrasting material.

Valencia almonds and raisins are a noted export.

The valance, or valence, the short curtain round the frame or canopy of a bed, has no connection with the Spanish university city. Its name is thought to derive from an old French verb, *valer*, to descend or fall.

Valtellina of Valtellina. The Lombardy river and valley of Valtellina extends from the valley of the Upper Adda to Lake Como, south of the Swiss border.

The province is famous for red wines and delicate white wines prized for their bouquet. Valtellina, of a light straw colour, is named after the district, and other noted varieties are Grumello, Inferno, Sassella and Frecciarossa which, in white, yellow and red types, is grown on the hills of Casteggio.

Vau de Vire of Vaudeville. The ancient town of Vire in Normandy, in the department of Calvados, claims the ruins of a 12th-century castle built by Henry I of England. The unexpected connection with Vaudeville arose through the 15th-century activities of Olivier Basselin, a fuller, of Vire. This poet composed or resuscitated drinking songs and convivial verse that rapidly spread through France and beyond. They were referred to as *Chansons du Vau de Vire*; songs of the Vire valley, which river enters the sea near Mont St. Michel.

Vaudeville was first a play in which dialogue and narrative were interspersed with songs. It gradually became synonymous with the normal British music-hall bill, with perhaps more accent on verbal and vocal acts than upon the extraneous novelties frequently presented to-day.

Vaudeville enjoyed a great following in the United States, largely through the efforts of B. F. Keith who, after a brilliant success in Boston in the eighties of last century, established a chain of theatres presenting vaudeville throughout the United States.

It became one of the most important factors in U.S. theatrical life and many stars of the legitimate theatre and of the films graduated in it. The vaudeville interests had a considerable part in the formation of the leading film and radio organizations.

Venice of Venice glass, Venetian blind, etc. The great Italian city and seaport of Venice is built largely on piles on over a hundred small islands. The city is laced with canals and connected to the mainland by a railway viaduct. Its glass has been famous for centuries and Titian and Giorgione are among the many old masters of the Venetian School.

Venice glasses, a term applied to the drinking vessels of the Middle Ages, most of which, in their finest quality, were made in Venice, were said to shiver to fragments when poison was placed in them. Byron (1788–1824) refers to the tradition in *The Two Foscari*.

Venetian blinds, once widely used in Britain and still seen, consisted of horizontal slats of wood that could be turned to admit or exclude the light.

The Venetian window properly has three separate openings.

The spirally painted poles used for street decorations are known as Venetian poles or masts.

Venetian carpets were of worsted, a striped pattern being most characteristic. The city produced a famous pointed lace.

Venice was the city of the Bridge of Sighs. The phrase is still used in many connections without knowledge of its origin. The bridge connected the Palace of the Doge with the State prisons. Across it the condemned were led to punishment.

Byron refers to it in *Childe Harold* and Thomas Hood published a popular poem with the title in 1846.

The decorative, lamp-adorned bridge across the Library of the Institute of Chartered Accountants, in Moorgate, London, is known as "The Bridge of Sighs."

Via Dolorosa of Via Dolorosa. The way or road of sorrows is an expression widely current to describe a passage through pain; physical, mental or spiritual. The Via Dolorosa was the way of Christ from the Mount of Olives to Golgotha and His Crucifixion. It was about a mile in length.

The adjective, meaning painful, anguished, derives from the Latin and is seen in dolour, dolorous, etc.

Swinburne (1837–1909) addresses his poem *Dolores* to "Our Lady of Pain."

Vichy-les-Bains of Vichy Water. The French town of Vichy-les-Bains, in southern France, on the river Allier, is a famous watering place. It is noted for its tonic water, which was widely exported, and for the less tonic effects of the French Government there during the German occupation of France in the Second World War.

Wall Street of Wall Street. The great U.S. banking centre of New York has become by name the term for U.S. financial opinion and commercial market reaction. The first Bank of New York, which was in operation five years before the United States Constitution was adopted, moved to Wall Street from George's Square (now Pearl Street).

Wall Street was also the site for many years of the sub Treasury of the United States.

Ware of the Great Bed of Ware. The Hertfordshire town of Ware, near the county town, once housed and is still associated with a bed of abnormal dimensions cited frequently in literature. It was said to belong to the Earl of Warwick, the 15th-century "kingmaker," but other authorities regard it as Elizabethan. It is a four-poster, 11 ft. 9 in. square with ornate frontal pillars and a massive carved canopy.

At one time it was exhibited in Rye House, Hertfordshire, but it is now in the Victoria and Albert Museum.

"As many lies as will lie in thy sheet of paper, although the sheet were big enough for the bed of Ware."
Twelfth Night, iii. 2.

"Oh, a mighty large bed; bigger by half than the great bed at Ware—ten thousand people may lie in it together, and never feel one another."
The Recruiting Officer,
George Farquhar (1678–1707).

The Ware strain is one of the most famous breeds of spaniels.

Waterloo of "To meet his Waterloo." Waterloo is a village a few miles south of Brussels, famous for the defeat there of Napoleon by the Duke of Wellington in 1815. The phrase "To meet his Waterloo," with varia-

tions, implies final and irrevocable defeat, particularly defeat for a hitherto triumphant person or cause.

Waterloo is one of the great London railway termini. Waterloo Bridge, over the Thames, was the oldest and by many considered the finest of stone bridges. It was replaced, in 1945, by the London County Council because dangerous settlements necessitated almost complete demolition and reconstruction. The architect of the new bridge, one of the modern sights of London, was Sir Giles Gilbert Scott, O.M.

Waterloo Cup, the "Derby" of dog coursing, is run annually at Altcar in February. It takes its name from the fact that it was founded, in 1836, by the sporting owner of the Waterloo Hotel, Liverpool, who gave the cup.

Wembley of Wembley. The Middlesex district of Wembley, near Harrow-on-the-Hill, first became nationally known through the staging there of the British Empire Exhibition in 1924–5. The vast stadium, accommodating 100,000, became the scene of the Football Association Cup Final and as such the synonym of professional football supremacy. The first final was staged there in 1923. It had previously been held at the Crystal Palace, Manchester (1915), Chelsea (1920–22).

Wembley Stadium has also been the site of football internationals, the Rugby League Cup Finals, the Olympic Games (1948) and other great sporting events.

Wensleydale of Wensleydale cheese. Part of valley of the Ure, in the North Riding of Yorkshire, near Jervaulx Abbey is known as Wensleydale. It is a beauty spot with many historic associations.

The district has given its name to

the noted blue mould cheese, and to a distinctive breed of long-coated sheep.

Whitechapel of "To play White-chapel." The east London district of Whitechapel, which includes the Tower of London and the London Hospital, was associated in the past with a polyglot population which included many aliens.

Whitechapel play in cards, particularly in whist, described a mean or unsportsmanlike procedure. The term was also used for the system of leading from a one card suit in order to trump in; and to the practice of playing master cards in reverse order —queen, king, ace.

A light-wheel sprung cart, familiar among travelling salesmen in the district, was known as a Whitechapel cart and the name was also perpetuated in the phrase "a White-chapel shave," which was not a shave at all but the application of powder to hide the growth. Most of the allusions imply a shoddy subterfuge no longer typical of the district.

Whitehall of Whitehall. The term Whitehall, the name of the impressive thoroughfare between Trafalgar Square, London, and the Houses of Parliament, is used as a synonym for Government officialdom and administration.

The street passes through the site of the main courtyard of the White-hall Palace, built in the reign of Henry III.

The Horse Guards, the Admiralty, the Treasury and the War Office are among the many imposing Whitehall buildings. Downing Street (*q.v.*), which includes the residence of the Prime Minister, leads off Whitehall. Many famous statues and monuments are centred on its great span, including Lutyens' Cenotaph, which is the focus of the Remembrance Day anniversary commemorations of the First World War.

Charles I was beheaded in front of the Palace of Whitehall.

White House of the White House. Internationally "The White House" stands for United States Presidential opinion. It is the official residence of the President, in Washington, Columbia, the capital of the United States and the seat of the U.S. Federal Government. The City received its charter in 1802 and George Washington, who had entrusted the planning of the great city to a French engineer, Major Pierre L'Enfant, who had served in the Revolutionary War, laid the corner stone of the White House. It and the Capitol occupy the sites originally planned for them.

The White House, which is 170 ft. long, was built between 1792 and 1799 from plans by James Hoban, who was influenced in his design by the home of the Duke of Leinster, near Dublin.

It has been painted white only since 1814, to hide fire marks following the capture of the city and the partial destruction of the House.

It was remodelled in 1902–3 and has been the scene of many famous conferences.

Wigan of Wigan. The sturdy, canvas-like material known as wigan, and used principally for stiffening, is named from the original place of manufacture, the Lancashire town of Wigan. It lies on both banks of the river Douglas. It still supports a textile industry and has a large commerce in coal, chemicals, etc.

Wilton of Wilton carpets. Carpet manufacture has brought fame to Wilton, the town in Wiltshire, west of Salisbury, since Tudor days. The county name is derived from it as Wilton was an episcopal see until the 11th century and was the capital of Wessex.

A century ago its carpet industry was increased by accessions from Axminster (*q.v.*). Wilton worsted carpets are frequently referred to as Velvet Pile, a reference to the long loops which are cut when the sharp weaving wires are withdrawn, leaving a full pile which may be sheared to secure evenness.

Wimbledon of Wimbledon.

Wimbledon is synonymous with tennis, and is its Mecca; occupying the place that Lord's claims in cricket.

This is due to the presence in the Surrey borough of the headquarters of the All-England Lawn Tennis Club. Success in its annual championships bestows the hall-mark of world fame and all the great players have appeared there.

The Lawn Tennis Championship was launched in 1877 by a number of men who were interested in rackets and tennis. The venture gave a new status to the game, clarified the varying codes of play and gradually assumed governing powers. The first championship, open to the amateurs of the world, was advertised in June, 1877, with two prizes. There were twenty-two entries. The first champion was Spencer W. Gore. The first American contestants appeared in 1883. The next year a Ladies' Championship was introduced. It attracted thirteen entries and Miss M. Watson won the title.

In 1907 the Prince of Wales, afterwards George V, bestowed the first royal patronage upon the Wimbledon championships.

The New Wimbledon, which holds nearly 20,000, was opened by King George V on June 26, 1922.

Winchester of the Winchester.

The standard bottle containing just under half a gallon, is known as the Winchester "quart" from the Hampshire cathedral city. Winchester was made the capital of England by the Saxon kings of Wessex, and the weights and measures of the district were gradually adopted as standard. The Winchester is used extensively in chemical and allied industries. The discrepancy between description and actual present day measures is not confined to the Winchester quart.

In the north of England it is still customary to talk about a "gill" when a half-pint is implied. So a quart in those times meant half a gallon. In mediæval times there were two gallons in normal use, the beer gallon—which approximated to the present gallon of 160 fluid ounces, and the wine gallon (the Winchester one) measuring 133¼ fluid ounces. This latter quantity went across the Atlantic with the early settlers, and the U.S. gallon of to-day (128 fluid ounces) is very little different from it.

The Standard Weights, the Yard and the Pound, are now in the keeping of the Standards Department of the Board of Trade, London.

The originals are walled up in the Houses of Parliament and are only used for comparison at long intervals.

There is a Standard Yard in the pavement of Trafalgar Square on the north (National Gallery) side for public reference.

The gallon is based upon the pound. The Weights and Measures Act of 1878 defines it as the volume of ten standard pounds of distilled water weighed in air against brass weights. Both water and air are required to be at 62° F., with the barometer at 30 inches.

Winchester College was founded by William of Wykeham in the 14th century. Its scholars are known as Wykehamists.

The Winchester rifle, used particularly in big-game hunting, is named not from the city but after its American inventor.

Windsor of the House of Windsor, Windsor chairs, etc.

The Berkshire borough of Windsor, on the Thames, is chiefly known for its Royal residence, Windsor Castle. William the Conqueror first built upon the imposing site, but in the 14th century and later under Elizabeth, the castle began to assume its present magnificence. It includes the famous St. George's Chapel.

Windsor Town Hall was built by

Wren and the church of St. John the Baptist includes notable carving by Grinling Gibbons.

The town was once noted for many famous inns, among which The Garter was mentioned frequently by Shakespeare.

The Royal Family adopted the title of the House of Windsor in 1917. It had previously been known, from the accession of Edward VII, as the House of Saxe-Coburg. In Queen Victoria's reign, back to the time of George I, it had been styled the House of Hanover.

The Knights of Windsor were founded by Edward III in 1349. The Most Noble Order of the Garter was created with them and the association continues to this day.

One of the six Heralds is known as the Windsor Herald. The English College of Arms, to which he is attached, was established by Richard III.

The Windsor chairs, with and without arms, were popular in the late 18th and early 19th centuries. They were all wood; strong, comfortable and their hooped backs and absence of "corners" made them popular in small rooms and cottages. Some of the later designs of these "stick-back" chairs incorporated a Prince of Wales' feathers design in splat, or central back support. They were also known as White Wycombes, from one of their chief places of manufacture in Buckinghamshire. Many were made in Wales.

A brown scented soap was also known as Brown Windsor.

Witney of Witney blankets. The Oxfordshire market town of Witney, 10 miles from the County town and situated on the Windrush, is noted for its blanket manufacture. The use of the term Witney for blankets manufactured there only, is protected by law. Blankets are, in fact, manufactured extensively in Yorkshire, Scotland and in the United States. Some, of a very fine texture, come from India.

Witney also manufactures gloves and other woollen goods.

The name blanket is said by some to derive from the Old French *blanquette*, and by others from the discoverer, one Thomas Blanket, who noticed the protective warmth of the woollen waste about his warehouse and exploited it by manufacturing the first blankets.

The term "wet blanket" for a dismal, oppressive person, derives from the extinguishing, damping or blanketing qualities of the article.

An illegitimate child is sometimes referred to as one born "on the wrong side of the blanket."

Worcester of Worcester Sauce, Pottery, Pearmain, etc. Worcester, the county town of Worcestershire, is an ancient cathedral city which has been the seat of a bishop since the 7th century.

Worcester sauce is manufactured here and the famous Royal Worcester Porcelain Works, founded in the 18th century, are supported by potteries.

The City, inseparably associated with Sir Edward Elgar, houses the noted Three Choirs Festival. The other sites are Hereford and Gloucester.

The substantial fruit growing industry of the county is recorded in the popular apple known as the Worcester Pearmain. The name probably has associations with Parma (*q.v.*), the northern province of Italy.

Worstead of Worsted. The woollen yarn known as worsted, and used extensively for suitings and dress fabrics, takes its name from the place of original manufacture, the Norfolk village of Worstead. It was a market town in the days when the wool industry flourished in Norfolk and Suffolk.

Worsted, particularly embroidered, was a noted material for bed hangings and as early as the 15th century worsted beds were often specifically named in the bequests of the rich.

Since the Second World War active efforts have been made to revive the ancient industry and many of the present inhabitants are direct descendants of the Flemish weavers.

X

Xerez of Sherry. Xerez, now known as Jeréz de la Frontera, is a town of Southern Spain, in the province of Cadiz, due south of Seville. It is famous for its vineyards and is also an important market for livestock and produce.

Sherry, which takes its name from the town, was originally known as sherris. The wine, most of which is fortified, has many flavours and many colours, ranging from light straw to dark brown. (See *Bristol.*)

The fortifying of a wine means the addition of wine spirit which increases alcoholic strength, checks the normal process and can be used to control sweetness.

A feature of the manufacture of sherry—which is extensively recommended by the medical profession in Spain as a restorative—is the treading in of burnt local earth which is sprinkled on the pulp.

Falstaff, in *2 Henry IV, iv. 3*, says: "A good sherris-sack hath a two-fold operation in it. It ascends me into the brain; dries me there all the foolish and dull and crudy vapours which environ it; makes it appre- hensive, quick, forgetive, full of nimble fiery and delectable shapes; which, deliver'd o'er to the voice, the tongue, which is the birth, becomes excellent wit. The second property of your excellent sherris is, the warming of the blood; which, before cold and settled, left the liver white and pale, which is the badge of pusil- lanimity and cowardice: but the sherris warms it and makes it course from the inwards to the parts ex- treme . . . and then the vital com- moners and inland petty spirits muster me all to their captain, the heart, who, great and puffed up with this retinue, doth any deed of cour- age; and this valour comes of sherris. . . . Hereof comes it that Prince Harry is valiant; for the cold blood he did naturally inherit of his father, he hath, like lean, sterile, and bare land, manured, husbanded, and tilled, with excellent endeavour of drinking good and good store of fertile sherris, that he is become very hot and valiant. If I had a thousand sons, the first human principle I would teach them should be, to forswear thin potations and to addict themselves to sack."

Y

Yorkshire of Yorker, "To come Yorkshire," etc. The great northern county of Yorkshire is said to have supplied the first bowler in professional cricket to exploit the ball that pitches immediately under the bat, now known as a Yorker.

The expression "To come Yorkshire" implies a cheating, over-reaching and over-confident attitude.

It is countered by "I'se Yorkshire, too," a tribute to the traditional canniness of the north-countrymen.

A Yorkist was an adherent to the White Rose during the 15th-century Wars of the Roses.

Yorkshire pudding is a famous local dish, served with roast beef and also as a separate course.

Z

Zion (Sion) of Zion. Zion, meaning sunny, was the name of a south-western hill of Jerusalem. David took it and it was called "the city of David" (*1 Chron. xi. 5–7*). His tabernacle was placed there. The name is also used in the Bible for Jerusalem and, in hymnology and present-day writings, for the heavenly Jerusalem or the kingdom of heaven. A Zion is also still a name for a Non-conformist chapel.

The Zionists are those who advocate the colonizing of Palestine by Jews.

Zoar of Zoar. The word zoar, signifying a place of refuge, a sanctuary, is still in use in religious and allied writings. The reference is from Zoah, a small town near Sodom (*q.v.*), where Lot and his daughters took refuge (*Gen. xix. 22–23*). It was formerly named Bela.

INDEX